LIGHTER
RED

ROSÉ

		64 G **Pz** Pinot Noir: NZ	72 R **Rd** Ribero del Duero	80 **Pt** Priorat	88 **Cs** Cabernet Sauvignon	97 G **Cg** Carignan

| 57 R **Ct** Chianti | 65 R **Ps** Pic St-Loup | 73 G **Ma** Malbec | 81 R **Bd** Bandol | 89 **Sy** Syrah | 98 R **Sh** Shiraz |

46 S **Wz** White Zinfandel

| 58 G **Bb** Barbera | 66 G **M** Merlot | 74 R **Cô** Côtes du Rhône | 82 R **Cp** Châteauneuf-du-Pape | 90 **Ce** Côte-Rôtie | 99 G **Zi** Zinfandel |

| 47 G **Gb** Grenache | 52 **Bj** Beaujolais | 59 G **Pm** Pinot Meunier | 67 R **St** St-Émilion | 75 G **Te** Tempranillo | 83 R **Ci** Cinsault | 91 **Du** Durif | 100 R **Pr** Primitivo |

| 48 R **Nv** Navarra | 53 G **Gm** Gamay | 60 R **By** Burgundy | 68 R **Rj** Rioja | 76 R **Bs** Barbaresco | 84 G **Gr** Grenache | 92 R **Ba** Barolo | 101 R **Pv** Petit Verdot |

| 49 R **Ra** Rosé d'Anjou | 54 R **Do** Dolcetto | 61 G **Pn** Pinot Noir | 69 G **Sg** Sangiovese | 77 G **Lg** Languedoc | 85 R **Ne** Nebbiolo | 93 R **Mv** Mourvèdre | 102 R **Ag** Aglianico |

| 50 R **Pd** Pays d'Oc | 55 R **Va** Valpolicella | 62 R **Mp** Montepulciano | 70 G **Br** Brunello | 78 G **Pi** Pinotage | 86 R **Na** Nero d'Avola | 94 R **Ca** Cahors | 103 G **Ng** Negroamaro |

| 51 R **Pc** Provence | 56 G **Bf** Blaufränkisch | 63 R **Cn** Chinon | 71 R **Cm** Carmenère | 79 R **Bx** Bordeaux | 87 G **Cf** Cabernet Franc | 95 R **Mé** Médoc | 104 G **Ta** Tannat |

110 R **Ch** Champagne	111 R **La** Lambrusco	112 S **Ss** Sparkling Shiraz
116 R **Sa** Sauternes	117 R **Bu** Banyuls	118 R **My** Maury
124 R **Rp** Ruby Port	125 R **Lp** Late-bottled Vintage Port	126 R **Tp** Tawny Port
		127 R **Vp** Vintage Port

You can never take what you love too seriously...

The Periodic Table Series

Periodically, we're all geeks about the things we love, and the Periodic Table Series has been created to celebrate this universal fact.

Inspired by the Periodic Table of Chemical Elements*, our experts have applied scientific logic to an eclectic range of subjects that regularly baffle beginners and fire up fans. The outcome of this experiment is the essential guide you hold in your hand.

Geeky? Absolutely.
Hugely satisfying? Categorically.

*The Periodic Table of Chemical Elements orders all the known matter that makes up our world, from hydrogen to helium, by chemical properties and behavior to give scientists a handy overview of a rather complex subject.

Molly,
I love you so much
they haven't even invented the maths yet.

THE
PERIODIC
TABLE OF

WINE

SARAH
ROWLANDS

Editor: David Cashion
Design Manager: Devin Grosz
Production Manager: Kathleen Gaffney

Library of Congress Control Number: 2016946246

ISBN: 978-1-4197-2408-4

Printed and bound in the United States
10 9 8 7 6 5 4 3 2 1

Abrams Image books are available at special discounts
when purchased in quantity for premiums and promotions
as well as fundraising or educational use. Special editions
can also be created to specification. For details, contact
specialsales@abramsbooks.com or the address below.

ABRAMS The Art of Books
115 West 18th Street, New York, NY 10011
abramsbooks.com

Contents

The Periodic Table of
WINE

FRUIT &
SPICE

FLORAL

GREEN &
MINERAL

1 G **C** Chardonnay: oaked			17 G **Fu** Furmint		28 R **Pp** Picpoul de Pinet	34 R **So** Soave	40 G **Mt** Müller-Thurgau
2 R **Pl** Pessac-Léognan	7 G **Gw** Gewürtraminer	12 G **Mu** Muscat	18 R **Vy** Vouvray	23 G **Mc** Muscadet	29 G **Fi** Fiano	35 G **Vd** Verdejo	41 G **Po** Pinot Grigio
3 G **Sé** Sémillon	8 G **Pg** Pinot Gris	13 G **Vi** Viognier	19 R **Ri** Riesling: Alsace or OZ	24 R **Cl** Chablis	30 G **Cb** Chenin Blanc	36 G **Vm** Vermentino	42 G **Al** Albariño
4 G **Mr** Marsanne	9 G **To** Torrontés	14 G **Sb** Sauvignon Blanc	20 G **Ar** Arneis	25 R **Sc** Sancerre	31 G **Vo** Verdelho	37 R **Rs** Riesling: Mosel	43 G **Pa** Parellada
5 R **Mn** Mâcon	10 G **Ro** Roussanne	15 G **Cu** Chardonnay: unoaked	21 G **Ga** Gavi	26 R **Gd** Greco di Tufo	32 G **Fa** Falanghina	38 R **Fr** Frascati	44 G **Ve** Verdicchio
6 G **Sv** Sauvignon Blanc: NZ	11 G **Pb** Pinot Blanc	16 G **Ay** Assyrtiko	22 G **Co** Cortese	27 G **Gv** Grüner Veltliner	33 R **Or** Orvieto	39 G **Tr** Trebbiano	45 R **Vv** Vinho Verde

SPARKLING

105 R **As** Asti	106 G **Mo** Moscato	107 R **Pe** Prosecco	108 R **Cv** Cava	109 R **Cr** Crémant

SWEET

		113 R **Iw** Icewine	114 R **Vs** Vin Santo	115 R **Tk** Tokaji

FORTIFIED

119 R **Fs** Fino Sherry	120 R **Ol** Oloroso Sherry	121 R **Md** Madeira	122 R **Rm** Rutherglen Muscat	123 G **Px** Pedro Ximénez

→

96 R **Am** Amarone

64 G **Pz** Pinot Noir: NZ	72 R **Rd** Ribero del Duero	80 R **Pt** Priorat	88 G **Cs** Cabernet Sauvignon	97 G **Cg** Carignan

57 R **Ct** Chianti	65 R **Ps** Pic St-Loup	73 G **Ma** Malbec	81 R **Bd** Bandol	89 G **Sy** Syrah	98 G **Sh** Shiraz

6 S **Wz** White Zinfandel		58 R **Bb** Barbera	66 G **M** Merlot	74 R **Cô** Côtes du Rhône	82 R **Cp** Châteauneuf-du-Pape	90 R **Ce** Côte-Rôtie	99 G **Zi** Zinfandel

7 G **Gb** Grenache	52 R **Bj** Beaujolais	59 G **Pm** Pinot Meunier	67 R **St** St-Émilion	75 G **Te** Tempranillo	83 G **Ci** Cinsault	91 G **Du** Durif	100 G **Pr** Primitivo

48 R **Nv** Navarra	53 G **Gm** Gamay	60 R **By** Burgundy	68 R **Rj** Rioja	76 R **Bs** Barbaresco	84 G **Gr** Grenache	92 R **Ba** Barolo	101 G **Pv** Petit Verdot

49 R **Ra** Rosé d'Anjou	54 R **Do** Dolcetto	61 R **Pn** Pinot Noir	69 R **Sg** Sangiovese	77 R **Lg** Languedoc	85 R **Ne** Nebbiolo	93 R **Mv** Mourvèdre	102 G **Ag** Aglianico

50 R **Pd** Pays d'Oc	55 R **Va** Valpolicella	62 G **Mp** Montepulciano	70 R **Br** Brunello	78 G **Pi** Pinotage	86 G **Na** Nero d'Avola	94 R **Ca** Cahors	103 G **Ng** Negroamaro

51 R **Pc** Provence	56 G **Bf** Blaufränkisch	63 R **Cn** Chinon	71 G **Cm** Carmenère	79 R **Bx** Bordeaux	87 G **Cf** Cabernet Franc	95 R **Mé** Médoc	104 G **Ta** Tannat

110 R **Ch** Champagne	111 G **La** Lambrusco	112 S **Ss** Sparkling Shiraz

116 R **Sa** Sauternes	117 R **Bu** Banyuls	118 R **My** Maury

124 R **Rp** Ruby Port	125 R **Lp** Late-bottled Vintage Port	126 R **Tp** Tawny Port	127 R **Vp** Vintage Port

ELEMENT KEY
TOP LEFT: ELEMENT NUMBER
TOP RIGHT: TYPE OF WINE
Grape variety (G)
Region/Appellation (R)
Style (S)

→

Introduction

Welcome to *The Periodic Table of Wine*. The table has been designed to give a visual overview of how different styles of the world's most popular wines roughly relate to one another. The descriptions later in the book contain more details about the elements of the table.

Dip in and dip out. Use the table practically and get family and friends together to smell and taste wines. Use it as a fun way to gain a deeper understanding of wine attributes, grapes, and regions. See if you agree with the relationships. Where does your wine sit? Open more than one wine at a time by asking your friends to bring a different bottle. Use all your senses—sight, smell, and taste, in that order—to notice the differences. Decide which wine you think has the fuller body, or is the fruitiest. Is it spicy or floral, or does it taste "greener" like herbs, or like minerals such as stones or chalk? Does your wine sit right in the middle of things? Add a rating to indicate how much you liked each wine you tasted and you could find that a pattern emerges, revealing that your favorite style(s) rest in particular areas of the table.

It is not really surprising that there are so many different wines available, but this can make choosing wine confusing. A little like chefs, winemakers all have their own recipes, numerous processes, and various techniques they use in production, from the way the grapes are grown and picked to every step of winemaking. Different grapes grow in different countries too. On top of this, the soil, climate, the vintage (the year a wine was made), and the age of the vines all affect how the final wine in the bottle looks, smells, and tastes. Sometimes even neighboring vineyards make wines with varying characteristics, and each commands a different price.

Knowing what is behind the name on a label is a big help in understanding what the wine in a particular bottle will taste like. For this reason, the table represents a bringing together of the most common names found on wine labels and relates them by their general characteristics (body, flavors, and aromas): hence the "style" of the wines. The descriptions contain information to clarify what each name means and should help you know what style of wine to expect. This should remove some of the questions and uncertainty you might have about purchasing an unknown wine while increasing your buying confidence, which should lead you on to some delicious new discoveries. So pop a bottle into your shopping basket and start sipping and discovering.

If you know you already like a certain wine, find it in the table, either directly or via the index. The wines closest to it in the table (above, below, left, or right) are similar but have different styles you may also appreciate.

Remember: Wine is not an exact science, so additional wines to try are also suggested in each description. Some are way more adventurous than others, and you might enjoy "researching" those as well.

How the table works

Wine elements, at their most basic, can be divided either into "grape varieties" or "appellations"; you'll find that these are the most common way wines are sold around the world. These label names are key pieces of information that point toward what is in the bottle. Thus a label may show the grape variety that was used to make the wine—or varieties, if the bottle contains a "blend" or mix of more than one grape variety. Look for names like Chardonnay, Cabernet Sauvignon, Sauvignon Blanc, and Merlot. Alternatively, the wine might be labeled using a protected name known as an "appellation," under which wines from a defined region may be sold (see Old World/New World, page 11).

Not all wines are included, but the wines you are most likely to come across are. While they can influence style, brand names, winemakers, and vintages have not been included in the table, as they cannot always be found locally; plus, they represent an additional layer of detail within or behind a single element or building block of the table—but they can be explored further by delving within an element to reveal this deeper layer of diversity. Perhaps you would like to conduct your own research by tasting for yourself different wines that fall into one element. The elements of the table have been designed as a starting point for the enjoyment and understanding of wine, by giving a broad overview of how the main wines made around the world relate. The graphic representation is a simplified bringing together of a diverse subject to provide a good foundation upon which your wine knowledge can build.

The columns broadly illustrate how wines vary by the weight or the feel in the mouth when you taste them. This is called "body." "Full body" is heavier, giving a weightier feeling on the palate in the form of big, bold flavors, textures, and tannins (especially in red wines). Full-bodied wines can range from rustic to full of finesse or opulent, if you like. A powerful and elegant wine is a sign of quality, especially if it is also described as having "complexity," meaning lots of layers of lingering flavors. Wines that tend to be full-bodied are placed in the outside columns of the table. They are a good match for flavorful dishes. The wines toward the center of the table are lighter-bodied and more delicate on the palate—useful when looking for a neutral-tasting, refreshing drink. This subtler style is popular as an aperitif in hotter weather or sipped on its own, and it pairs well with lighter cuisine because neither overpowers the other.

The rows in the table give an indication of the general

types of flavors you might encounter in a wine. With practice (smelling and tasting), especially comparing different wines at the same time, distinguishing these attributes becomes easier. To begin with, focus on identifying whether a wine is young or fruity; only later should you try to identify the types of fruit you can taste. The more you practice, the better you'll get at identifying the various characteristics. When you start out, just remember that very few wines actually taste like grapes. Instead, you might spot flowers in your first wine, which places it more in the table's middle rows. Other aromas and flavors, such as herbs or minerals, would put a wine near the bottom of the table. Some wines have many of these traits, so could justifiably find themselves in a different row; however, they have been placed closer to their more usual features.

Always bear in mind that taste and smell are personal. We all taste and smell differently, so there is no "right" answer. You may find that you prefer one brand or winemaker over another, or that you prefer a particular wine due to the type of food you enjoy or the occasions when wine is drunk. It is OK to have these differences of opinion and create your own table. Some people are more inclined to taste bitter hints and might prefer softer, sweeter wines, whereas others might be better at tasting floral notes instead, so they would find these same wines too sweet. Likewise, wines taste different with and without food, so there is plenty of scope for experimentation here. Usually wines are drunk with food, so why not test out which wine you think is best with what you are eating? With a really good match, both the food and the wine should taste better.

Maybe you've already tasted wines from significant appellations: those defined winemaking regions that are usually controlled by strict local rules concerning the wines made within them. The labels will have names like Bordeaux, which is a French wine appellation; Rioja from Spain; or Chianti, which is from Italy. These popular and well-known places or regions give their names to admired wines that are often blends of more than one grape variety (but not always: Chablis is an appellation that allows only white wines made from 100 percent Chardonnay grapes to bear its name). The rules in each appellation govern, among other things, the variety of grape(s) that can be used in the wines that carry the appellation name on the label. Although *The Periodic Table of Wine* began with the idea of each entry being a single element, such as a grape variety, the idea of omitting anything on the basis that it wasn't "pure"— i.e., that it was a blend—seemed wrong and unhelpful. These "compound wines" are not "elements" in the strict sense, but they are crucial to include when mapping the world of wine.

Rosés have found a home in the center of the table, being neither red nor white but a combination of the two colors. However, rosé wines are not normally made from a mixture of red and white wines; instead, their pink color comes from the skin of red grapes. Typically the fleshy pulp inside the grape contains clear juice, and this juice is turned into wine, fermented by yeasts that eat the fruit's natural sugars, then convert them to alcohol. White wines are, in general, made by fermenting grape juice only. Red winemaking includes a period of time where the skins and clear juice mingle to add color, resulting in purple, ruby-red, or merely pale-garnet wines. Like red wines, rosés are made using red grapes, with the pink color usually the result of letting the grape juice and skins stay in contact for only a short time—a little like the way colors from a tea bag infuse into the water. The hue, style, weight, and texture of still rosés differ depending on the grape variety, as well as details of the infusion method used. Within the Periodic Table, rosés could have been distributed in and among the white and red table wines based on weight (light to full-bodied) and flavor characteristics. However, they would have been lost as an important category of still wines—and so, too, would the appreciation of just how varied pink wines are.

"Rare earth" elements

Three categories have been given separate rows because they are less likely to be drunk regularly and have qualities that make them either taste or feel different from still wines: sparkling, sweet, and fortified wines. They are often put into a separate section when you are buying wine too.

Sparkling wines have the extra dimension and texture created by their bubbles, sometimes called "mousse," as the bubbles in those that exhibit finesse create a smooth, almost creamy sensation. They need not be saved for a special occasion, though, so pop a cork and make any occasion special.

Sparkling wines contain all the elements of still wines and could easily form their own detailed table. They range from young, pale, *pétillant* (lightest of froth) or floral, frivolous, *frizzante* (with a little more fizz) fizzes through to the more edgy, fully effervescent, serious, and complex (lots of different layers of flavors and lingering length) bubblies and the richest, most creamily textured, all-honey-and-brioche vintage Champagnes.

Sparkling wines are also made in a variety of colors. They are mainly white wines, although the "white" can range from pale, almost water-white to a rich, deep, golden color. There are sparkling rosés, but only a few are the deepest of reds, such as Australia's classic berry-and-pepper-spiced sparkling Shiraz.

Some bubblies are made in the same way as Champagne via what is called (in the Champagne region only) the *méthode champenoise*—i.e., the Champagne method—or, outside the region, the *méthode traditionelle*, or the traditional method. These include French *crémant*, Spanish Cava, German Sekt, and Italian Franciacorta. Others, like Asti and Prosecco, both made in Italy, have their own methods, because experience has shown that different techniques work better with the grape varieties that grow in their regions, and help to bring out the grapes' fruit and perfumed, floral qualities.

All bubble-adding methods take time and skill, however, so sparkling wines tend to cost more than still wines. Wine can be carbonated in the same way that soda is: by adding carbon dioxide. While this is a much cheaper, quicker fix, it is not associated with any classic sparkling wine, and creates bursting bubbles that are quickly lost, and are not as fine nor as integrated with the texture and flavor of the wines involved.

Most wines, including sparkling, are dry—that is, "not sweet to the taste" in wine-world speak (rather than "not wet" in the rest of the world). "Off-dry" means only a suggestion of sweetness. "Medium" has a touch more noticeable sweetness, which usually comes from the natural sugars that were in the grapes when they were harvested rather than from added sugar.

Intense and concentrated sweet and fortified wines should not be overlooked, as their layers of flavor can linger on the palate. Discover the pale, bone-dry fino sherries with their flashes of salted almonds and green apples; apricot and stone-fruited dessert wines; and the opaque, inky, powerful dark cherries and chocolate of vintage ports. These are not your everyday wines of choice, but they may be areas to branch into. They are made using different techniques from those used in still wine—hence their diverse characteristics. Many could make a dessert on their own.

Again, even their sweetness is natural. The grape juice may have been concentrated in some way, such as by leaving the grapes on the vine longer so that they start to dry out or "raisin." Fermentation—changing the sugar in the grape juice to alcohol—can be stopped partway through the process, leaving some of this natural sweetness remaining in the finished wine. In fortified wines, this is achieved by adding neutral brandy partway through the fermentation to "fortify" (hence the name) the wine. Note: Not all fortified wines are sweet; some have a beguiling concentration wrapped in bone-dry elegance.

To choose your sweet and fortified wines, look for mouth-watering acidity, as that balances intensity and sweetness. As a style, these dessert wines can be refreshing and appreciated even by those who claim not to have a sweet tooth, and they make a heavenly match for cheese or pâté as well as desserts. If pairing wine with a dessert, pick a wine that is at least as sweet as the dessert. A heavier style of sweet wine matches more substantial cakes or pies, while a more delicate, maybe even floral, sweet wine works well with lighter fruit desserts. When pairing savory foods with sweet wines, go by the weight of the food and choose a similarly weighted sweet wine so that salty and fatty flavors from the food are balanced by the sugar and acidity from the wine.

How to use this book

Each element appears in this book following the table order—by column, running left to right across the table—and moves through the types of still wine—from whites to rosés then reds—followed by sparkling, then sweet wines, and finally fortified wines. Their entries describe the types of flavors, aromas, and other attributes you might find in your glass. You'll find food-matching hints here too. There may also be a comment on how they might vary by winemaker or region or how the wines could change with age.

The table is all columns and rows and straight lines, but in practice the boundaries are blurred; in reality you could zoom in further, say, into one grape variety or appellation, and make a new table that shows there is diversity and relationships across countries, regions, and even winemakers. This is something you might like to do in time. Some aspects that create this diversity and depth in wines follow.

The cells here are all the same size, although when it comes down to it, some wine elements are far more important than others, either because of history, volume consumed, or both. You may have come across some grapes already, as they are the most respected and recognizable grape varieties grown around the world. This is for good reason; historically, these leading international varieties have been valued for their ability to produce quality wines wherever they are grown, and in some regions they are reputed to produce the top wines in the world. They include reds such as cassis-laden Cabernet Sauvignon; softer, plummy Merlot; and more delicate Pinot Noir, plus whites such as versatile Chardonnay; aromatic Sauvignon Blanc; and fresh, zippy Riesling. These grapes are behind the labels of some of the most respected wine regions in the world, such as Bordeaux and Burgundy, but because they are used by so many winemakers they are readily found on most wine shelves in numerous places and prices from the most wallet-friendly upwards. Use this table as a springboard to try new wines made from international grape varieties as well as lesser-known grapes, and experiment with all that there is available.

Many wines, but not all, are made in a range of styles, which makes things more confusing. The table is necessarily a simplified representation that gives an overview of how wines relate. Differences could nudge a particular wine in a column one way or another, from middle, lighter-bodied styles to medium-weight, say, or even bump them into the full-bodied arena. This diverseness could be caused by variances in production techniques (such as using oak barrels); the temperature of grape juice at the time of fermentation creates different aromas, which can bring out a more floral side to a grape—or alternatively, a more fruity side. Letting vines grow fewer but more intensely flavored grapes also affects a wine's concentration and power, and variations in the vineyard express themselves in the final wine. Grapes like Pinot Noir are more likely to convey these aspects of origin. Perhaps you notice qualities in the glass you're tasting that might bump your particular wine into a different position: left or right, up or down. If you like it, make a note to look out for that type of characteristic next time you buy a wine.

Vintage is important for some wines, such as Bordeaux or Port, when wines made in a particular year are thought of as superior to others by taste or longevity potential. They may make the headlines, but they will cost more, and they tend to be less easily available. Zoom in and you are bound to find exceptions, like a particular winemaker who has bucked the general trend. Get an idea of what constitutes a good Bordeaux, for example, then check out vintage differences. For the majority of wines, however, vintage is less important; they are released ready to drink more or less straight away while still relatively young.

Some descriptions include remarks on how layers of flavor are added by using different winemaking techniques, which give a wine "complexity." Aging and other techniques mean that wine production can cost a bit more. There are good reasons for this, such as using better-quality grapes, more steps, or extra details in the process, plus the cost of barrels. These all manifest themselves in extra layers of lingering flavors that can make a wine more interesting. The description might comment on this if it could affect the wine.

Experiment. Taste a different wine, a different country of production, a different winemaker, a different grape variety. Be bold. Try a different color or style. You could find that by swapping one element—say, the winemaker or brand—you like a type of wine you thought you wouldn't. This can happen with all grapes and regions, but a classic example is Chardonnay, because this versatile, juicy, white grape is available in a huge gamut of styles and guises around the globe. Perhaps your first, unhappy experience was with a heavily oaked, super-ripe, full-bodied style of Chardonnay. However, sip a lighter more elegant Chablis or a Chardonnay made without using oak from a similarly cool vineyard elsewhere in the world and you could fall in love with this more refreshing style—made with the same golden grape. Or maybe a delicate, pale gold, *blanc de blancs* Champagne, with its apple-like notes, is just the Chardonnay for you? Liken it to coffee preferences; some people don't enjoy sugary, creamy coffee but love reviving black coffee. They're both still coffee—just made differently. Tasting wine "blind"—i.e., covering the labels so you don't know what you're drinking—helps remove preconceptions. Why not arrange a blind tasting with friends? They could each bring a bottle wrapped, and you could compare notes afterward.

Tasting notes

Wine terms have been kept to a minimum, since this is not meant to be a textbook. Some words that are regularly mentioned are worth expanding upon. If you don't know them, it will not affect what is most important, which is whether you like a wine. If you are familiar with them, however, this could help you work out why you like a style of wine and guide you toward what to look out for in the future. Some terms have been covered within the text already, but here are a few more:

**Old World/
New World:** Notice that some wines are named after the region in which they are made—think of wines like Rioja (in Spain), Chianti (Italy), Chablis and Bordeaux (both in France). These are long-standing, traditional names that define winemaking areas generally occurring in the "Old World": the more historic winemaking areas found mostly in Europe. The winemaking rules of each region specify the permitted grape varieties, so you would not be allowed to make a Bordeaux wine using Pinotage grapes, for instance, nor make and call it a "Bordeaux" even if you used permitted varieties but made it outside the region. Having a broad understanding of which grapes are behind an Old World appellation on a label is a significant step toward knowing what a wine will taste like. The table acts as a foundation here, without going

into the detail of the local rules.

Other wines are more simply the name of the grape variety in the bottle: for instance, juicy red Merlot or Malbec. These varietally labeled wines are more likely to have been made in the "New World"—i.e., outside Europe, in Chile, California, or Argentina, for instance. The classification "New World" doesn't mean there isn't a long history of winemaking in these places; it is a naming convention in wine—another detail that can make wine feel more complex and confusing than it needs to be. Knowing about grape varieties is still the easiest way of knowing what a wine might taste like. Increasingly, Old World wines are helping consumers by including the names of grape varieties on the label.

Acidity: Acidity is regularly mentioned, as it is needed to maintain freshness. When drinking a wine, acidity is what makes your mouth water. It is a key part of the structure of wine, giving it another dimension and bringing out its flavors. Acidity levels vary, depending a great deal on the grape variety, where it was grown, and how the wine is handled in the winery. Wines with high levels of acidity are made to accompany food, so if you find a wine style too lip-smacking and lemon-laced on its own, serve it with snacks or as part of a meal. Acidity is essential, a positive attribute in wine as in food, like tempting dishes making your mouth water in anticipation. Think of fruit that has gone off: it's a bit woolly and flat-tasting compared to a juicy, fresh segment or slice. In wine terms, acidity might be really racy, nervy, or edgy, more middle-of-the-road zesty, fresh, lively, or crisp and then sometimes delicate. An over-the-hill wine is flat, tired, out-of-date, lacking both fruit and good flavors with "flabby acidity." We don't wish to be drinking a dull old wine like that as there are far too many bright, fresh, juicy accessible wines to try.

Tannins: Tannin is found in red wines, including fortified ones such as Port. Tannin creates a drying sensation in the mouth, especially around the gums, and creates a feeling like an oversteeped cup of tea, but tannins are important as they are part of a balanced wine's structure. When too high, tannins can feel chewy. Tannic wines soften if drunk with cheese or meat. Decanting tannic wine also helps; this is simply pouring the wine into another bottle or jug to aerate it. If there are any bits, called sediment, at the bottom of the wine bottle, stop pouring before they transfer to the other container. For some wines with plenty of fruit flavors accompanying the tannins, keeping them longer or aging them before drinking tones down the tannins. Bitter or grippy tannins can be why some people stick with white wines, but not all tannins are unfriendly. Look for tannin-describing words like "velvety," "supple," "soft," and "silky," with "firm" being a good halfway house. Not all red wines have high tannins, either. Wines toward the middle of the table are lighter, lower-tannin, easier reds. Try those as a "starter red" if you usually choose whites. Better styles of reds have tannins that are more at one with the wine, or "integrated."

Some white wines also have tannins. They are inclined to be the fuller-bodied styles. As the skins are not usually used when making a white wine, the tannins here come from using oak barrels during the winemaking process and are more subtle than those in most red wines.

Oak: Oak, which is used in both red and white winemaking, adds cream, vanilla, and spice notes, especially cloves, and a touch of weightiness to a wine's texture. It can also impart smoky or toasted layers. Coconut nuances are a sign of American oak rather than French oak, and nutty tinges are an indication of long aging in oak. Newer and smaller barrels add more of these tones. The winemaker decides how much or little is required so as to balance, rather than overpower, the other flavors in the wine.

Not every wine would suit the qualities oak brings. It increases the cost of winemaking as well, so expect to pay more for a wine made using oak.

***Vieilles vignes* (VV):** The flavor and intensity of a wine can vary with the age of the vine on which the grapes grow. *Vieilles vignes*, "VV," or old vines bear fewer grapes than younger vines during each autumn harvest. In addition, they are more likely to be hand-picked instead of harvested by machine. The smaller volume of wine that results is more concentrated, and this is reflected in the wine's final characteristics. Expect a deeper, more intense-tasting, and often more complex wine with lingering qualities—and anticipate paying more for it.

Now, with full glasses in hand and your friends close by, go ahead and delight in all the multifaceted elements and compounds the world of wine has to offer.

Whites

Column 1

1 G **C** Chardonnay: oaked	
2 R **Pl** Pessac- Léognan	**7** G **Gw** Gewürztraminer
3 G **Sé** Sémillon	**8** G **Pg** Pinot Gris
4 G **Mr** Marsanne	**9** G **To** Torrontés
5 R **Mn** Mâcon	**10** G **Ro** Roussanne
6 G **Sv** Sauvignon Blanc: NZ	**11** G **Pb** Pinot Blanc

This column represents bold white wines that can have the greatest weight, texture, and flavor when you drink them. They might feel more viscous or rounder in the mouth—almost as if they were thicker. They may have more alcohol, so check the level on the label. Sometimes being fuller-bodied is due to the grape variety, or it may be because the grapes used to make the wine have been left to ripen for as long as they can; often it is attributable to the winemaker using methods that add weight to the wine, such as using oak, which adds a creamy texture or dimension.

If you like red wines, you may enjoy this style of white wine more than the lighter styles.

CHARDONNAY: OAKED

A famous, versatile, leading or international white grape variety that makes dry wines in many wine regions across the globe. The fatter, riper style of Chardonnay is often made in hotter regions, where the grapes mature fully. This element of the table represents the full-bodied version of Chardonnay, and these wines may have high alcohol levels. Here winemaking techniques are used that can add a buttery, vanilla, creamy edge and deep color to the final wine. Once overoaking masked the super-ripe New World fruit bombs of melon, mango, and tropical fruits. Now these Chardonnays are more restrained, better balanced and textured, with refreshing hints of spice such as ginger and cinnamon as well as toasty notes; the oak and fruit are working together in a more integrated manner. Aspirational white wines of Burgundy are subtly oaked, infusing them with gentle vanilla and cream notes. This fuller-bodied oaked style of Chardonnay is often suitable to keep, and as it ages it becomes more honeyed and nutty. (Another white grape, Pinot Blanc, can be similarly styled.) Full-bodied Chardonnays can pair well with dishes with cream sauce, and the finer examples are on restaurant wine lists around the globe. For those who prefer white to red wine, oaked Chardonnays can partner with roast dinners due to the range of accompaniments.

PESSAC-LÉOGNAN

An esteemed French wine region, or appellation, situated in the northern part of Graves, part of the Bordeaux winemaking region in southwest France. Wines from here are dry and rich, and can be mouth-watering whites (and also reds, but see Bordeaux). Whites are usually a blend of the white grapes Sauvignon Blanc and Sémillon plus sometimes a splash of Muscadelle, which adds an extra dimension as a suggestion of musky, floral perfume, and a splash of spice. When young, these pale, fresh, and lively blended whites are more subtle than a New Zealand Sauvignon Blanc and can have citrus, green apple, and fresh nectarine flavors. Premium blends are richer, with a fuller texture, but they are more expensive. They are made using some oak and age well, gradually turning more golden in color and developing a lusher, smoother texture accompanied by more complex, lingering exotic fruit flavors like mango and clementine, along with notes of honeyed beeswax, nuts, sweet spices, and soft leather. Be warned: they can be expensive. Alternatives for aged Pessac-Léognans include aged Chardonnays like Burgundy, and you could try riper and more alcoholic blends from the southern Rhône. Pair them with light game, hams, Asian dishes, roast pork, and creamy main courses.

SÉMILLON

A leading white grape variety with thin gold skins closely associated with Bordeaux in France, but also with Australia (where it loses the "é"), especially the Hunter Valley region. It can be used to make both interesting dry and succulent sweet wines with a variety of flavors and textures. It is often blended with Sauvignon Blanc and Muscadelle. Famously, it is the majority grape in the luscious, silky-textured, apricot, honey, and marmalade sweet wines of Sauternes in Bordeaux (see page 128). Both dry and sweet wines can age. The more affordable wines, as well as those from cooler climates or where the grapes were harvested when less ripe, have fresh flavors of lemon, apple, pear, and a touch of waxiness, plus white flowers. This style pairs well with bass and other seafood, herbs, and pasta. Sauvignon Blancs can be an alternative here. Aged Sémillons and those from warmer regions have richer flavors and aromas, such as mangos, peaches, figs, and ginger. They are more likely to be made using oak, and cost more. This maturation adds another layer of flavors like butter, vanilla, and a touch of smokiness; there may also be nuts and higher alcohol too. Richer versions are a good match for roast chicken, butternut squash, and mushroom risotto. Also try Pinot Gris, Chardonnay, and Viognier. Sémillon can be added to Chardonnay to make the wine zippier, fresher, and more affordable, so look for this blend as a midweek sipper.

MARSANNE

A weighty white grape variety found in French wines from the Rhône and farther south, and in a few other sun-kissed regions too. Often found blended with Roussanne, which adds heady perfume to the fruit, it is usually dry, with acidity levels that are not too high. It has a full-bodied, smooth texture in the mouth, with plentiful levels of exotic peach and melon fruit, honeysuckle, and alcohol. It can be almondy, quince-like, and honeyed, especially with age. Famous French wines are called names like St-Joseph, Crozes-Hermitage, and Hermitage, the most expensive. For more affordable Marsanne, try a white Côtes du Rhône or look for one from Languedoc-Roussillon, which might contain other grapes as well. Great with grilled food, butter sauces, and mildly spiced Asian meals. You might also like Chardonnay, Viognier, oaked white Riojas, and Pessac-Léognan.

MÂCON

Mâcon is a wine region in the south of Burgundy, France. It makes mostly white wines from Chardonnay grapes, with some red Gamay and Pinot Noir wines. Mâconnais white wines are straw-colored. (They can have more specific vineyard names, like Pouilly-Fuissé, which typically signifies a better-quality wine than simple Mâcon; Mâcon-Villages is halfway between.) They are dry and fresh with a full (especially in warmer vintages) to medium, rounded, smooth, honeyed texture plus white-flower flavors, citrus fruits, and perhaps a touch of crème fraîche. Premium versions are richer, with poise, and offer complexity plus depth of flavors balanced by elegance and minerality from the limestone soil. (Compare with Chablis wines from north of Burgundy, which are more acidic and linear in style.) Food-friendly pairings include finger food, dishes in creamy sauces, and risottos. They are often better with a touch of age as they soften and are more approachable, developing earthy mushroom notes. Refreshing red Mâcons are light and juicy with red-cherry and soft, red-fruit flavors; perfumed, with light tannins. Try with ham, terrines and pâtés, and savory pastries. The lively, elegant rosés are much harder to come across, though, and being similar to the reds of Mâcon, they pair well with cold cuts, couscous dishes, and quiche.

SAUVIGNON BLANC: NEW ZEALAND

Here the white Sauvignon Blanc grape is used in New Zealand to produce an important and popular zesty, pungent, but crowd-pleasing style of lively wine. Lots of sunshine, combined with cool climate plus time on the vines, provides vibrant notes of green pepper, gooseberry, plus the archetypal "cat's pee" or asparagus notes together with ripe flavors that sometimes merge into passion fruit and juicy lime zest. These Sauvignons usually have more weight in the mouth than their subtler cousins from Sancerre (France) and elsewhere. Often from New Zealand's Marlborough region, this well-loved wine style has only been around since the 1980s. It's youthful and usually made to drink in the year of production. Its punchiness means it can match stronger fish flavors like mackerel and creamy fish pie. Occasionally, Sauvignon Blancs are made with oak, which mellows and rounds out the wine, adding a creamy flavor and texture. This style is more likely to age. You might also like to try less aromatic Sémillons, Pinot Blancs, plus Viogniers and compare it with a more restrained Sancerre.

Column 2

1 **G** **C** Chardonnay: oaked		
2 **R** **Pl** Pessac-Léognan	**7** **G** **Gw** Gewürztraminer	**12** **G** **Mu** Muscat
3 **G** **Sé** Sémillon	**8** **G** **Pg** Pinot Gris	**13** **G** **Vi** Viognier
4 **G** **Mr** Marsanne	**9** **G** **To** Torrontés	**14** **G** **Sb** Sauvignon Blanc
5 **R** **Mn** Mâcon	**10** **G** **Ro** Roussanne	**15** **G** **Cu** Chardonnay: unoaked
6 **G** **Sv** Sauvignon Blanc: NZ	**11** **G** **Pb** Pinot Blanc	**16** **G** **Ay** Assyrtiko

These wines can be rich white wines similar to those in column 1; however, often the weight and texture are lower; plus, they may have aromatic characteristics created in the vineyard by leaving the grapes to hang or (less so) by using oak. Richer versions tend to cost more than lighter forms.

GEWÜRZTRAMINER

An aromatic white grape variety that grows best in cooler regions like Alsace in France (where it loses its "ü"), also in Germany for a slightly lighter style, while Chile makes affordable, uncomplicated versions. Prominent notes of lychee, rose petal, citrus to pineapple fruit occur in the ripest styles. Some can have ginger and other spicy hints, as well as a touch of smokiness; they tend to have a higher alcohol content and a weightier texture too. Serve these exotic wines cool to bring out the best of the medium acidity level, balanced with lychee, plus floral notes and a touch of residual sugar. German wines can be more subtle and delicate. This makes them a good introduction to this more blousy grape, as are better-value Chilean wines. Look out for *vendange tardive*, or "late harvest," grapes, which make dessert wines—great with fruit-based desserts. Pair with Thai and Moroccan food, especially spicy cuisine, takeout, and onion tart. If you want a white wine to match Thanksgiving dinner, an Alsace Gewürztraminer has enough weight to partner the turkey and trimmings; it's good with cilantro and coconut too: think of Thai curries. Other fruity, floral wines to try include Muscat/Moscato, Torrontés, and, for more acidity and fewer flowers, Riesling.

PINOT GRIS

This is the same white grape as Pinot Grigio. Pinot Gris is the more full-bodied version, found in Alsace,

Germany (as Grauburgunder and Ruländer), New Zealand, and Italy. Wines are richer, with a more viscous texture compared to straightforward Pinot Grigio. The grape is versatile, so wine styles range from unoaked and light, with fresh pear flesh and a touch of green herbs, to rich and honeyed, with flavors of riper (and even baked) pears. They can also contain stone-fruit flavors such as white peaches, a touch of sweet spice like ginger, hints of flowers, and cream from oak. Pinot Gris is also versatile with food; it can accompany a wide range of dishes, including lightly spicy Asian food, pork casserole, and hard cheeses (for sweet wines). Some wines, though harder to find, are made to age, like in Washington, where fermenting in oak barrels and adding a splash of Viognier gives creamy and aromatic wines. Pinot Gris is also made in sweet styles called *vendange tardive* (late harvest) wines, and the rare, more concentrated sweet Sélection des Grains Noble (SGN). Both match blue cheeses and fruit desserts. This is a grape to investigate further as it is quite different from its light, neutral, affordable cousin Pinot Grigio. Also try Pinot Blanc, Chardonnay, Sémillon, and Riesling.

TORRONTÉS

Argentina's signature perfumed white grape variety is mostly made for early, fresh drinking. These light-yellow, refreshing, exotic wines may surprise as they can smell sweet but taste dry. They can be rich with medium body and a pleasant weighty roundness in the mouth. You'll find floral aromas of jasmine and geranium coupled with fruit-salad flavors, green and herb hints like oregano plus citrus acidity (but not overly so) from lemon to more exotic lime. They can also be honeyed with pear and passion fruit. Usually not oaked, the wine shows pure fruit and flower flavors, but be warned: they can be 13 percent-plus ABV (alcohol by volume), to balance the complexity of flavors. Less expensive versions have less of the perfume, flavors, weight and complexity, but are nonetheless pleasant to sip. Serve chilled, paired with aromatic, lightly spiced Asian and Indian dishes and light fish flavors. This wine slips down easily as an aperitif or patio wine. Try also Gewürztraminer, peachier Viognier, grapier Muscat, and versatile Pinot Gris.

ROUSSANNE

A white grape whose traditional home is on the steep vineyard terraces of the northern Rhône. It is also found in rich, higher-alcohol, more affordable blends in the southern Rhône and other warmer regions in the world. It makes medium- to fuller-bodied, racy, floral, slightly exotic wines with hints of chamomile and herbs and a zesty grapefruit note. It is a versatile wine, so expect to find some versions with more bracing acidity and mineral hints, and others that are much richer and more voluptuous, with nutty notes. It is often blended with Marsanne for a more complete style. Strength tends to be 13 percent-plus ABV (alcohol by volume) to match its flavors. It is food-friendly so pairs with an assortment of dishes, including exotic cuisine, seafood such as lobster and shrimp, cheeses, nuts, and spices. Other blends with Chardonnay and Viognier can yield perfumed, richly textured wines. If you enjoy this, also try Pinot Gris, Viognier, and the less floral Pinot Blanc.

PINOT BLANC

A white wine grape used mainly for elegant, pale-yellow, slightly creamy dry wines. It can be hard to come by, as only small amounts are made in Alsace in northeast France, Italy, Germany, plus Oregon. Usually soft and rounded with peach hints, plus a range of apple flavors (green to red). Typically made without oak, which allows mineral notes to come through.

Oaked versions are bolder and tend to have hints of nuts (almonds) and more cream or yeasty notes. A good wine for appetizers, simple main-course dishes like omelets, and buffets. (Sometimes it is made into sparkling and sweet wines.) It is even harder to find the northwest Italian version, called Pinot Bianco. This is a lighter, zingier wine so accompanies lemony dishes like chicken, and is a good match for fennel. You could also try easier-to-find Chardonnay and Pinot Gris. Pinot Blanc is not quite so acidic as some wines, hence the softness. This variety can be overlooked but is one to try if you prefer wines that are not too sharp.

Column 3

		17 G **Fu** Furmint
7 G **Gw** Gewürztraminer	12 G **Mu** Muscat	18 R **Vy** Vouvray
8 G **Pg** Pinot Gris	13 G **Vi** Viognier	19 G **Ri** Riesling: Alsace or OZ
9 G **To** Torrontés	14 G **Sb** Sauvignon Blanc	20 G **Ar** Arneis
10 G **Ro** Roussanne	15 G **Cu** Chardonnay: unoaked	21 R **Ga** Gavi
11 G **Pb** Pinot Blanc	16 G **Ay** Assyrtiko	22 G **Co** Cortese

Here the white wines are moving toward medium- to lighter-bodied, forming a large group within white wines. Flavors are less bold.

MUSCAT

The name for a family of grapes found in the world's warmer, sun-blessed regions. Known as Moscato and Zibibbo (a touch lighter) in Italy, and Moscatel in Spain, Muscat is an ancient grape variety; there are many strains of the grape and many styles of wines are made from them, but all have grapiness and exotic floral notes at heart. Muscat wines in all their styles tend to be orange blossom–scented. The grape makes elegant dry white wines, some with a steelier style and touches of herbs, others richer with more texture and roundness in the mouth, but always with the perfumed flowers and fresh fruit-salad tones. Serve chilled as aperitifs, or with spicy dishes, chicken, and cheese. Try Argentinian Torrontés, along with Gewürztraminer wines. See also Moscato and the low-alcohol (5–7.5 percent ABV) Asti in the sparkling wine section. Sweeter, more viscous dessert wines such as Muscat de Beaumes-de-Venise and Muscat de Lunel—both from France—are tinged with gold. They pair well with fruit salads and warmed peaches. Though fortified, around 15 percent ABV (alcohol by volume), their flavors are still delicate and floral. They are youthful and should be drunk young and chilled. Richer, darker, and more honeyed, with marmalade splashes, Klein Constantia's Vin de Constance, from South Africa, suits fruit cakes and cooked fruits. Australian Rutherglen Muscats, also known as "stickies," are darker again, with more dried than fresh fruit and spices. Look out for other Muscat sweeties that are similarly styled but more affordable wines made in California and Chile.

VIOGNIER

A peachy white grape variety whose traditional home is in France's northern Rhône. It is typically bottled on its own, but is also used in blends in some places because of the character it can bring to other, more subtle grape varieties. It is lush, full-bodied, and intensely perfumed, with notes of honeysuckle and apricot. You can find wines made farther south in France that include Viognier as part of a blend; it is also found in Australia, New Zealand, South Africa, California, and Chile. Not too acidic, it can be softer-styled. Viogniers from Australia can have a touch more texture and zest—lemon and lime hints—and some have sweet spice and pears. Alcohol can be around 14 percent ABV (alcohol by volume) to balance the exotic flavors. They are best served chilled. Premium versions, meant to be drunk aged, are generous, rich, and complex, with exotic tropical and citrus fruits. They can include creamy notes from the dead yeast cells (known as the "lees") that remain in a wine after fermentation is complete. The more common youthful wines match Asian dishes or delicate curries; others pair well with smoked salmon and lemon chicken. A much more floral wine swap is Gewürztraminer or Torrontés. You might also like Marsanne and Roussanne wines.

SAUVIGNON BLANC

Sauvignon Blanc is a highly aromatic white grape that makes fresh, lively wines throughout the world. It is generally a crowd-pleaser and a good introduction to white wine. See New Zealand for an assertive style, and France (Sancerre) for a subtle, more mineral taste. The grape grows well in a variety of climates and soils, mirrored in the wines. Youthful versions are more readily available, such as the more restrained herby, grassy examples from cooler Bordeaux, with styles from warmer regions offering riper flavors of gooseberry, asparagus, perhaps meadow flowers, and even tropical-fruit notes like guava. South Africa, Chile, and Argentina make good-value, drinkable Sauvignons typically in a style that is halfway between France and New Zealand, in bottles furnished with a screw cap as these refreshing whites are made to be drunk young and served chilled. In the United States, Sauvignon Blanc can be called Fumé Blanc. Great as an aperitif and with green salads, picnics, and buffets. Occasionally a Sauvignon has lees (dead yeast cells left over from fermentation) stirred in while it is being made, which adds a cream or crème fraîche layer—think yogurt tartness—as well as more body and roundness. Occasionally Sauvignons are made using oak barrels, which gives them more depth of creamy, vanilla flavors and an ability to age, but always with a higher price tag (these wines tend to have a cork). Pair them with richer food, such as pork or fish in a white sauce.

CHARDONNAY: UNOAKED

15   G

C

Chardonnay: unoaked

Popular and adaptable, this leading, versatile white grape variety makes a leaner, fresher, zippier style when unoaked, moving toward steely acidity. Unoaked Chardonnays tend to be paler, crisper, more mineral and refreshing than their richer, rounder, oaked siblings, with greater elegance. Flavors in this livelier style are more fresh citrus, even green, with crisp apple and pear tones. The best grapes for unoaked Chardonnays are grown in cooler regions, sometimes near coasts, and at altitude—or at least away from the equator. In these locations grapes take longer to ripen, so the best have extra time to develop a more complex, layered flavor profile. More affordable versions are straightforward or simple, but cheap versions can be a little thin and disappointing. (See also Chablis, page 39.) Serve chilled with summer foods, seafood, and pasta. Other wines to try include Gavi and Cortese from Italy, Sauvignon

Blanc for more greenness and aromatics, and Greece's Assyrtiko for more sharpness. If you moved on from Chardonnay because of the oak, then it's time to revisit this livelier style.

ASSYRTIKO

Greece's underappreciated white grape makes a refreshing, medium-bodied, bone-dry wine, with floral and steely notes. It also has aging potential. Sun imbues this wine with high alcohol. The best, from the volcanic Santorini, give pretty floral/honeysuckle and citrus-filled wines. Those from the oldest vines add more intensity to the racy, zesty, lemony acidity and include a salty tang, with mineral hints from the volcanic soils. Some are blended with Sauvignon Blanc; others age gently for a short time in oak and have a further soft, creamy note and rounder texture. Serve lightly chilled to accompany meze, plus pasta and other dishes with white sauces; fish, shellfish, and white meats. Younger versions are more austere. With age they mellow, and honeyed flavors develop. (There are some sweet versions too.) Try also Sauvignon Blanc, Chablis, and Cortese, or for a little more spice, find an older Grüner Veltliner.

Column 4

	17 G **Fu** Furmint	
12 G **Mu** Muscat	18 R **Vy** Vouvray	23 G **Mc** Muscadet
13 G **Vi** Viognier	19 G **Ri** Riesling: Alsace or OZ	24 R **Cl** Chablis
14 G **Sb** Sauvignon Blanc	20 G **Ar** Arneis	25 R **Sc** Sancerre
15 G **Cu** Chardonnay: unoaked	21 R **Ga** Gavi	26 R **Gd** Greco di Tufo
16 G **Ay** Assyrtiko	22 G **Co** Cortese	27 G **Gv** Grüner Veltliner

Wines here are becoming zingier and still have character on top of lemony freshness. Oak is becoming less likely to be used from here on in.

FURMINT

A white grape usually grown in Hungary and used to make the world-famous, complex, and long-lived sweet botrytised white wine called Tokaji (made slightly differently than Sauternes in Bordeaux, France). Dry Furmints have fruit, spices, and mineral tones like a combination of aromatic Sauvignon Blanc and racy, mineral Riesling, with the ability to be happy if oak is used in production. You should find good weight in this crisp, dry, smooth-textured wine whose depth of flavors include lime rind, ripe pears, light nuts, and sometimes sweet spices like ginger, as well as preserved lemons and a touch of smokiness—especially where oak is used. Furmints are becoming easier to find outside Hungary, and it is worthwhile searching for them. Dry Furmints are food-friendly—well worth trying if you come across one on a wine list. A versatile partner, it can match dishes from risotto and pork to lightly spiced food. Sweet Tokaji is delicious on its own, or with light fruit cake, apricot tart, and blue cheese salads. If you like dry Furmint, try Gavi, Cortese, aged Chardonnays, racy Chenin Blanc, and Roussanne for a riper, fruitier edge. Alternatives for sweet Tokaji include Sauternes, Vin de Constance, Montbazillac, and late-harvest wines made from Furmint, Sémillon, or Sauvignon Blanc.

VOUVRAY

Famous prestigious French region situated in the Loire Valley making white wines mainly from the versatile Chenin Blanc grape. The appellation (and wine) is named after the commune of Vouvray, roughly in the center of the Loire wine district. Refreshing wines are produced in all styles and levels of sweetness. This can be confusing as Vouvray covers bone-dry, sparkling, and sweeter wines, from the medium-sweet *demi-secs* to luscious, mouth-watering, fully sweet, golden dessert wines reflecting the varying weather in this northerly region. It always has high, vibrant, even racy acidity. Most Vouvrays are drunk young, as they are typically light- to medium-bodied. Expect to find apple, quince, and lemon juice flavors, along with blossom notes. The chalk and flint soils along the Loire River can impart a chalky, mineral layer. Premium-priced Vouvrays age well, adding depth and weight to the texture, and may be made using some oak. Their flavors become more exotic: apples become baked apricot; blossom notes morph into honeysuckle, and there are honey and classically lanolin/waxy notes too. These wines tend to have more texture, aromatics, and balance than lower-priced South African Chenin Blancs (see Chenin Blanc, page 44). Sparkling Vouvray, made in the same way as Champagne, is good value and pairs well with sushi and lightly fried food. Try dry styles, chilled, with fish and savory soufflés, while off-dry wines match pork belly, spicy Indian cuisine, and crab. Tarte tatin is heaven with a sweet Vouvray. Other Chenin Blanc wines you might like are from the nearby Montlouis appellation, or try wines made from Sauvignon Blanc (Touraine, Sancerre) or the less acidic Pinot Gris.

RIESLING: FROM ALSACE OR AUSTRALIA

A perfumed white grape variety with intense, crisp acidity and clean flavors. Wines are dry, medium-bodied, and certainly weightier than those from Germany's Mosel region but still retain steely acidity. Made without oak, they demonstrate a purity of style and fruit flavors. In Australia and New Zealand, citrus notes, especially lime, feature heavily. Think lime marmalade, or lime cordial with zest, plus a touch of green apple and blossom. Some can be sherbet-y in their zippiness. Alsace Rieslings feel fatter than Australian versions. Wines are light yellow to green in color, but darken with age and develop stone and gasoline/mineral notes earlier in life compared to Mosel Rieslings. Premium wines are more generous in all attributes and will age better, although they cost more. Rieslings are food-friendly and pair well with duck, grilled shrimp, and ceviche, as their acidity is ideal to balance richer foods.

ARNEIS

20	G
Ar	
Arneis	

A white Italian grape variety. It makes dry, herbaceous, pretty wines with gentle floral aromas mingled with hints of orchard fruits. Other flavors include pears and apples, peach pits, and mineral notes like stones, plus a splash of citrus and lime—soft and not too acidic. Arneis wines are usually made to drink young, so look out for recent vintages. Medium-bodied, the best are riper, aromatic, and have floral notes similar to those in Viognier or Pinot Gris. They're even rich and viscous in the mouth, and aromas can be more delicate than flavors. More neutral, refreshing styles have herbiness. Arneis is used solely to make the white wines of Italy's Roero Arneis appellation, and it features as the majority grape in some white wines from the Langhe region as well. Great chilled with simple Italian cuisine like spaghetti, garlic and olive oil dishes, and Waldorf salad. If you like this style, you might also enjoy riper versions of Pouilly-Fumé from the Loire, peachier Viogniers, appley Chenin Blancs, and more zesty, grapefruity Gavis.

GAVI

A town in Piedmont, northern Italy, that also gives its name to crisp, food-friendly, medium-bodied, herby, floral, zesty, dry—sometimes bone-dry—white wines made exclusively from Cortese grapes. A range of qualities is made, most of which are best drunk young and usually made without oak influence. Richer versions can have peachy, honeydew melon aromatics, hints of nuts with grapefruit on the finish, plus some mineral qualities. They are the perfect accompaniment to grilled seafood, chicken in white sauce with fresh herbs, and as an aperitif. Try Arneis, also from Italy, or dry Furmint, a more steely Chablis, Fiano, or a white Côtes du Rhône for something riper and more alcoholic.

CORTESE

A white northwest Italian grape, occasionally found as a named variety, although you are more likely to see it as a crisp, zippy, food-friendly, dry Gavi wine. It is also used as part of a blend in other Italian white wines (and a tiny amount is made into wine in Australia) and is similar to, but not quite as sharp as, breezy Picpouls or steely Chablis, but with more to it than Pinot Grigio. The best are full of citrus/lemon freshness, lime aromatics with a grapefruit finish, and perhaps a touch of stone-like minerals. Higher-priced wines have more body, complexity, and length of flavor. This is the ideal partner, served chilled, for fish dishes, grilled shrimp, salads, lightly poached chicken, and pork-based meals. For a less acidic Italian wine, sip Arneis, or try a more tropical, nutty Fiano from southern Italy. This is a refreshing grape variety to try if you haven't already.

Column 5

17 G **Fu** Furmint		**28** R **Pp** Picpoul de Pinet
18 R **Vy** Vouvray	**23** G **Mc** Muscadet	**29** G **Fi** Fiano
19 G **Ri** Riesling: Alsace or OZ	**24** R **Cl** Chablis	**30** G **Cb** Chenin Blanc
20 G **Ar** Arneis	**25** R **Sc** Sancerre	**31** G **Vo** Verdelho
21 R **Ga** Gavi	**26** R **Gd** Greco di Tufo	**32** G **Fa** Falanghina
22 G **Co** Cortese	**27** G **Gv** Grüner Veltliner	**33** R **Or** Orvieto

White wines are becoming lighter in body and often color too. These popular styles are suitable for everyday drinking as well as pairing with lighter cuisine, but can come in refreshing, lingering, richer guises with some seriously excellent-quality wines hidden among them. Frequently they are made in a zingy, zesty style.

MUSCADET

Muscadet is the name of a place, a white grape, and a light French white wine from around the city of Nantes, found at the western Atlantic end of the Loire Valley. These tangy citrus wines with a touch of grapefruit are made from the Melon de Bourgogne, aka Muscadet, grape (which has nothing to do with flowery Muscat and Muscadelle white grapes). Some Muscadet wines are straightforward and fairly neutral so this wine can be underrated, but well-made versions make a refreshing sipper on a hot day to accompany a light snack. Best to look for the more characterful Muscadet-Sèvre-et-Maine *sur lie* wines. These have been left "on the lees" (dead yeast cells left over from fermentation) over the winter after harvest. This adds a layer of creamy notes, plus provides more texture and depth in the wines. Think of a splash of crème fraîche. These wines should be clean and fresh-tasting, with apple and citrus notes, mineral hints from the chalky soils, creamy if *sur lie*, sometimes with a touch of salinity. Typically no oak is used. Muscadet is made to be drunk young and fresh, and immediately after opening to feel the extra dimension of a tingly spritz on the tongue. A classic to accompany seafood, especially fruits de mer, plus light, herby salads; also makes a great summer sipper. Try instead Pinot Grigio, Frascati, steely Chablis, zippy Picpoul de Pinet, and Spanish Parellada wines.

CHABLIS

A white-wine-only appellation in northern Burgundy, France, named after the town of Chablis, making elegant, mouth-watering, and steely wines solely from the versatile Chardonnay grape. Chablis wines exist in four quality levels. As we move up the ladder, production volumes drop, prices increase, and the wines become more concentrated, complex, and lingering. All should be vibrant, with a steel girder of mouth-watering acidity providing a refreshing linearity in the mouth, rather than the rounded, fatter feeling of some Chardonnays. Look for the most affordable Petit Chablis, but try Chablis (the largest category) if your purse stretches to it, with sharp lemon peel, white blossom, and chalk nuances. Next is *premier cru* Chablis and finally the pinnacle and rarest *grand cru* Chablis, a complex wine with long, ripe, peach and baked-lemon flavors and the ability to age; it may also have seen oak in its production. Alcohol is usually around medium levels. Chablis can be found on practically every wine list and is classic served chilled to accompany oysters, shellfish, and white fish, other seafood dishes, and the likes of mushroom risotto. Try instead unoaked Burgundian Chardonnays, zippy Picpoul de Pinet also with high acidity, Gavi from Italy, and, with a touch of spice, Grüner Veltliner from Austria.

SANCERRE

A celebrated hilly wine district and appellation named after the small town located in central France overlooking the Loire River, famous for its high-quality, crisp, mineral, and aromatic dry white Sauvignon Blanc wines found on many a wine list. (A tiny proportion of Sancerre wines are delicate reds and rosés made from Pinot Noir grapes.) Wines are medium-bodied, with medium alcohol levels. Bracing acidity, although still elegant, accompanies white-blossom perfume, with subtle hints of gooseberries, lemons, and leafy nettles plus chalk and a tangy finish. Pair a white Sancerre with goat's-milk cheese, shellfish, asparagus, plus onion and other vegetarian tarts. This is a classy summer sipper. New Zealand Sauvignons tend to be fuller-bodied, with more punchy aromatics and riper green flavors. South African Sauvignons are a good halfway point. Pouilly-Fumé, from the opposite side of the Loire river to Sancerre, has more flinty tones due to the different soil. Try also Spanish Albariño, Greek whites and southern Italian whites like Greco di Tufo, and, with more apple and pear notes, Fiano.

GRECO DI TUFO

Greco is a widely planted, medium-bodied, perfumed, and sometimes herbal white grape from southern Italy, grown mostly in Campania and also Puglia. There are several Grecos, the most well-known from Tufo, i.e., Greco di Tufo. It can appear in affordable, light, simple blends from the same region; look for Irpinia and Sannio. Usually dry, some sweet and sparkling examples are made, though these are harder to find. Wines are fresh and typically made to drink young. Flavors include pear, green plum, and peach, sometimes with a salty tang or a touch of bitter almond. A richer alternative to Sauvignon Blanc. A food-friendly and popular wine worth discovering if you haven't already. Serve chilled with pasta, shrimp, seafood (especially sea bass), and deep-fried beignets or falafel. Try also other southern Italian whites.

GRÜNER VELTLINER

A versatile white grape that is becoming more readily available. It is the signature white grape of Austria, a country whose wines, in general, are likely to be high quality. Grüner Veltliner has refreshing high acidity, which lingers in the more concentrated wines. Younger,

fresher styles to sip are dry, crisp, light, and citrusy—
think lime, lemon, and grapefruit—with notes of green
pepper. As the wines become richer they typically
develop more weight and fullness in the mouth, still
with steely freshness plus more texture, perfume,
mineral hints, and characteristic touches of white
pepper. This style is harder to find and costs more
but tends to be age-worthy. Some are tangy with an
aromatic hint of dill. In addition, flavors of nuts, cream,
and honey also occur when oak is used. Some Grüner
Veltliners can age like the best wines of Burgundy, and
plantings are expanding around the globe. You may
come across Grüner Veltliner wines with higher levels
of sweetness, though these are less common. Grüner
Veltliner is an alternative to Sauvignon Blanc, but also
try Chardonnay, Pinot Gris, and Greco di Tufo from
Italy. Grüner Veltliner is food-friendly, so makes a good
choice for a range of dishes, including lighter meats,
spicy meals, creamy cheeses, and green vegetables
(even artichokes).

Column 6

	28 R **Pp** Picpoul de Pinet	**34** R **So** Soave
23 G **Mc** Muscadet	**29** G **Fi** Fiano	**35** G **Vd** Verdejo
24 R **Cl** Chablis	**30** G **Cb** Chenin Blanc	**36** G **Vm** Vermentino
25 R **Sc** Sancerre	**31** G **Vo** Verdelho	**37** G **Rs** Riesling: Mosel
26 R **Gd** Greco di Tufo	**32** G **Fa** Falanghina	**38** R **Fr** Frascati
27 G **Gv** Grüner Veltliner	**33** R **Or** Orvieto	**39** G **Tr** Trebbiano

Some white wines here have lip-smacking zinginess, though now the table is moving into wines that can be more neutral, easy-drinking, and popular, especially when made in large volumes. These columns of white wines are very interchangeable, so this is a part of the table open to lots of experimentation.

PICPOUL DE PINET

A coastal appellation in the far south of France making light, high-acidity, really fresh white wines with a lemony zing from the Picpoul grape grown in the region surrounding the small French village of Pinet. Pale lemon-yellow and usually found in tall, slim, green bottles, Picpoul de Pinet is similar to Muscadet, but with more floral notes, like white blossom, bracing lemon and lime citrus, and a splash of salinity, pear, and apple. Some have a touch of peppery spices; others, green herbs. A bone-dry, no-oak, breezy white wine that should be drunk young while at its freshest alongside seafood such as mackerel or oysters and Mediterranean cuisine; it is a surprisingly terrific match for fish and chips. A zingy swap for Muscadets, Sauvignon Blancs, Grüner Veltliners, and Vinho Verdes.

FIANO

An ancient southern Italian white grape, grown mainly in Campania, especially Fiano d'Avellino, plus Sicily, some other Italian regions, and a little is made in Australia. Mainly produced as a varietal wine, though sometimes blended, as in Irpinia wines that are bianco (white). It can withstand the southern heat and still yield a vibrant, pure, and intensely fruity wine. Alcohol levels can be medium to high. Not as aromatic as Greco di Tufo, Fiano can have minerality if grown on poor, volcanic soils at altitude. Look for label comments about cool-temperature fermentation and expect candied citrus and grapefruit notes, apple, chamomile, or white-blossom tones, with perhaps apricot, honey and nut flavors, and a waxy texture in the best. Serve chilled with seafood, white meats, and cheeses. Try also Greco di Tufo, Sauvignon Blanc, or a lighter Frascati.

CHENIN BLANC: FROM THE NEW WORLD

A leading versatile white grape variety known for its high levels of refreshing acidity. It can make dry, sweet, and sparkling styles of honey- and quince-flavored wines, some with the capacity to age. South Africa has the largest plantings of Chenin Blanc in the New World. Its dry wines are more exotically fruit-flavored (think pineapple, melon, and yellow plum) compared to the French wines, which show more of a warm apple tang. Value wines are easy-drinking and made without oak, so are "pure," if perhaps on the neutral side. Terms like "old-vine," "bush vine," and "lees [dead yeast cells] stirring" on the label indicate higher-quality grapes are used. Wines are still pure, though with more concentrated apple, citrus, and a touch of lanolin flavor, added texture and weight in the mouth, complexity, and length. This style is more likely to be made with oak, which adds a layer of vanilla, though levels vary so explore. Chenin Blanc is food-friendly; match the weight of wine to the weight of the food. The lightest match salads and white fish: try sea bass. Sweeter styles accompany tarte tatin. See also Vouvray for Chenin Blanc wines from France. Zippy wine swaps include pure, fresh Riesling, lighter Albariños, Chablis for steeliness, or oaked Chardonnay for vanilla and tropical flavors as a swap for the richer style of Chenin.

31	G
Vo	
Verdelho	

VERDELHO

A white grape variety originally grown in Portugal to make straw-colored, versatile, light, affordable wines (though full-bodied wines are produced, especially in Australia). Wines can smell and taste of hints of grapes. Blending Verdelho with better-known grapes like Sauvignon Blanc and Sémillon results in a range of styles and weights, and can be a means of making a lighter, more affordable wine. Be guided by the label. Blending with local Portuguese varieties creates an everyday style. European Verdelhos are lighter, more subtle and elegant than New World wines, juicy, with fruit salad and citrus flavors. Australian versions tend to be more green, with flavors like lime and honeysuckle, and can be softened or have vanilla notes, depending on how the wine was made. This quaffable wine is drinkable without food, and pairs well with tapas, appetizers, or spicy Asian food. You could also try Godello, Albariño, a lighter style of Chardonnay, or more intense Grüner Veltliner. Riesling is generally more acidic and Sancerres have more mineral notes and finesse.

FALANGHINA

A southern-Italian white grape variety found mainly around Naples in Campania. Its high acidity is useful, yielding fresh, crisp sippers with zesty aromatics. When grown at altitude Falanghinas can be light-bodied and elegant, with leafy notes, plus a touch of honey and tangerine on the finish. The volcanic soil adds a mineral layer of chalk or stone. Enjoy with pasta and pizza, fish, white meats, poultry, and as a good aperitif. More flavor than Pinot Grigio, plus an alternative to Sauvignon Blanc, Soave, Chablis, and other lighter, crisp wines at the leafy end of the spectrum. Worth discovering if you haven't already.

33	R
Or	
Orvieto	

ORVIETO

A commune in Umbria gives its name to crisp, youthful, central Italian white wine usually made from a blend of grapes. Usually dry, although sweeter styles are made but mainly drunk locally, and pale. Those labeled "classico" tend to have more character. They are light-bodied, easy-drinking, inexpensive, and sometimes neutral. Look for a peachy perfume, citrus notes, and hints of crunchy green apples; richer versions include a touch of green pears, fresh peaches, and maybe white flowers. Alcohol levels tend not to be high so Orvieto makes a good aperitif and is a crowd-pleaser. Orvietos pair well with simple dishes such as salads, white meats, and lighter seafood. Try also Frascati, simple Pinot Grigio and Muscadet, zesty Gavi for something with more weight, and steely Chablis.

Column 7

28 R **Pp** Picpoul de Pinet	**34** R **So** Soave	**40** G **Mt** Müller-Thurgau
29 G **Fi** Fiano	**35** G **Vd** Verdejo	**41** G **Po** Pinot Grigio
30 G **Cb** Chenin Blanc	**36** G **Vm** Vermentino	**42** G **Al** Albariño
31 G **Vo** Verdelho	**37** G **Rs** Riesling: Mosel	**43** G **Pa** Parellada
32 G **Fa** Falanghina	**38** R **Fr** Frascati	**44** G **Ve** Verdicchio
33 R **Or** Orvieto	**39** G **Tr** Trebbiano	**45** R **Vv** Vinho Verde

This column is a mix of lighter grape varieties and wines that are suitable for aperitifs, sipping in the sunshine, and serving alongside lighter cuisine like salads and seafood. If you prefer wines without oak, you are likely to find them here.

SOAVE

More commonly an elegant, easy-drinking, dry, white Italian wine from the Veneto region in northeast Italy made mainly from Garganega grapes, but with Trebbiano and other white varieties added too. (Some sweet Soave is produced, which is a lighter style than Sauternes.) Usually affordable, this is a pale, lemon-green wine with fresh, citrus acidity; it may be fairly neutral, so is popular as a light aperitif. More succulent wines include apricot tones, a stone-like mineral hit from the volcanic soil, green herbal tinges with waxy weight, and a creamy, soft texture, which can be due to using some oak in the production process; these are more expensive. Try it with creamy chicken or chicken Kiev, pasta and gratin dishes, or serve it with a few green olives. You may also like Grechetto, Pinot Grigio and Orvieto.

VERDEJO

A white grape from Rueda in northwest Spain that makes delicate, youthful, and fresh wines often blended with some Sauvignon Blanc. Wines are light to medium-bodied, crisp with softness along with refreshing citrus notes like lemon, sometimes grapefruit and lime, also green apple and mineral touches, and they can have light nutty hints too—easy-drinking with suggestions of floral and herbaceous notes. The better wines have more texture, like a touch of cream and richness, and notes of honey. Pairs well with appetizers and lighter main courses. Alternatively, why not try a Pinot Gris with its similar texture, or a lighter Spanish white like Airén or Viura?

VERMENTINO

A white grape variety that makes pale, straw-colored, green-tinged zippy wines in Sardinia. It is the same as Rolle in southern France, and Pigato in northern Italy. Increasingly it is successfully made in Australia. It makes delicious dry, lemon, green-apple-y, and peachy wines that are fresh, zippy, and unoaked to retain freshness; these are wines to drink young. Sometimes they include a touch of citrus leaf, basil, or white-blossom aromas and a clean mineral note. Pigato styles tend to be more aromatic. This is one to try if you like unoaked light to medium white wines, such as simple Pinot Grigio, the weightier dazzling Gavi, and white, peachy, light Orvieto. Delicious with Mediterranean vegetables, salty snacks, and seafood. Other wines to sip include Albariño, Verdicchio, and, for something even zippier, Picpoul de Pinet.

RIESLING: MOSEL

An aromatic white grape here it is grown on steep slopes by the winding Mosel River in Germany. It is light-bodied, easy-drinking, and low in alcohol: around 8 percent ABV. Flavors are pure and mouth-watering. Usually pale with green hints, with green apples, white peach, and piquancy, these clean wines are made without oak influence. Most are designed for early drinking. A range of sweetness levels is available, from off-dry to bone-dry. Drier styles tend to be more alcoholic, but some labels are less helpful than others as far as taste profile is concerned, so persevere. Even *Halbtrocken*, or "half-dry" wines, where a little unfermented sugar has been left in, appear drier, so are not cloying, because the grape variety contains high levels of acidity. For those that can age, with a much richer, fuller-bodied, premium-priced style, that interesting mineral note described as "gasoline-like" develops later. The light wines are food-friendly and ideal chilled as a summer lunchtime or evening aperitif, their purity pairing well with Japanese and Chinese cuisine. *Halbtrocken* wines are good with Thai dinners. This is an interesting grape to investigate further. Also try Müller-Thurgau (which is neutral in comparison), Albariño, Chablis, Muscadet, and Grüner Veltliner for other refreshing wines. Compare with Riesling from Alsace, Australia, and New Zealand.

FRASCATI

A region in Italy near Rome that gives its name to a famous—and ancient—pale-yellow, light, lower-alcohol, dry, easy-drinking, and crisp white wine. It is made from a mix of several grapes, including Trebbiano and Malvasia. This popular, affordable crowd-pleaser has delicate apple and lemon flavors and is refreshing, sometimes with hints of wildflowers or grassiness and almonds. Serve young and chilled as a good match for seafood, salads, and simple pasta dishes. If you like Frascati you could try other Italian wines, such as Pinot Grigio, Orvieto, Soave, and the more zippy Verdicchio and Vermentino for a tangier style. You could also expand into unoaked Chardonnays and Sauvignon Blancs from Europe (which are more subtle than those from New Zealand).

TREBBIANO

A white grape mainly found in Italy and France that is often not shown on a label as it is blended to make white wines of many names. In France it makes dry, crisp, relatively neutral-tasting, pale, affordable wines for immediate consumption, showing simple citrus and green-apple flavors, a light to medium body, and similar alcohol levels. In Italy it may have more color and zest, but wines are still dry, bright, and fruity. Trebbiano d'Abruzzo is a crisp wine with a light floral bouquet. The grape can also form part of Orvieto and Frascati, so you could try these. (See, too, Vin Santo, a sweet Italian wine.) These wines are crowd-pleasers for parties, which also work well with antipasti, simple pasta and seafood meals, and light lunches. A good wine swap for Italian Pinot Grigio.

Column 8

34 R	40 G	46 S
So Soave	**Mt** Müller-Thurgau	**Wz** White Zinfandel

35 G	41 G	47 G
Vd Verdejo	**Po** Pinot Grigio	**Gb** Grenache

36 G	42 G	48 R
Vm Vermentino	**Al** Albariño	**Nv** Navarra

37 G	43 G	49 R
Rs Riesling: Mosel	**Pa** Parellada	**Ra** Rosé d'Anjou

38 R	44 G	50 R
Fr Frascati	**Ve** Verdicchio	**Pd** Pays d'Oc

39 G	45 R	51 R
Tr Trebbiano	**Vv** Vinho Verde	**Pc** Provence

This final column of white wines contains quaffable light and neutral styles ideal for beginner white-wine drinkers, with the more mineral styles being the most zesty.

MÜLLER-THURGAU

A white grape variety used chiefly in Germany to make wines which, at their core, are light, drinkable, and simple with sweet peach aromas and fruity flavors. Usually these neutral wines are low in acidity and youthful, so buy them for immediate drinking. Often off-dry, they can be part of a lower-alcohol blend of delicate grapes, like Liebfraumilch, found in slim blue bottles, which might also call the grape Rivaner or Riesling-Sylvaner. An easy, uncomplicated drink chilled on its own, served with snacks, or with light salads and meals. It can be a gentle introduction to white wine. You can also try Mosel Riesling for a more lingering glassful with greater finesse (look for "*Kabinett*" on the label); Pinot Grigio for a drier, more neutral style; Soave, or the similarly off-dry white Zinfandel from the United States; and Portuguese rosés.

PINOT GRIGIO

A popular white grape variety that makes good-value, quaffable, dry wines mainly from Italy that are clean, simple, neutral, and ideal as aperitifs. Within this crowd-pleasing style you could find subtle citrus fruits, apple, and green pear notes, refreshing acidity, and alcohol levels on the lower to medium side. Occasionally made into a rosé, which is similar to the white but with a touch of red fruit such as cranberry and red cherry. For everyday dining, drink chilled with pasta, grilled dishes, quiche, and buffet foods. Also try Soave, Frascati, and, for rosé, a dry Provence or off-dry Portuguese or US Zinfandel blush wine. See also Pinot Gris, the same grape variety but made in a richer style.

ALBARIÑO

Dry, white local grape from Galicia, in northwest Spain. Wines are pale green to lemon-colored, and light-bodied with lemony acidity. Albariño can be blended with other light grapes. Usually zippy, zesty, and refreshing without oak and made to be drunk young. Look for some light, floral aromatics. The best, more jasmine-perfumed, shows hints of white peaches, fresh apricots, and almonds, and there is a trend toward this higher-quality style. Great chilled with seafood, light fish, mussels in garlic and herb butter, and salads. In northern Portugal this grape is called Alvarinho; see Vinho Verde (page 55). Plus, look out for Rías Baixas. Try also Muscadet and mouth-watering Picpoul de Pinet.

PARELLADA

A Spanish white grape used mainly in Cava but also to good effect in still dry wines. Usually delicate, it can sometimes be aromatic. A still wine, it is predominantly available in uncomplicated, fresh, youthful, drinkable, affordable light wines. Look for lemon, lime, white flowers, white nectarine, and sometimes herbs in your glass, though often the wine is simple and easy-drinking. Drink immediately, chilled, any time of day. Good for informal lunches with dishes such as rice, fish, and shellfish. Its moderate alcohol makes it ideal as an aperitif in the summer. Try also simple Pinot Grigio, herby Orvieto, Muscadet, and Frascati.

VERDICCHIO

A white central Italian grape variety that makes dry, bright, lively, citrusy (lemon and lime), fresh, light-styled wines that can have floral notes and greenish tinges in the color—hence the name. Look out for nutty almond hints. The style is usually affordable, uncomplicated, and made to consume young, with medium alcohol. A small number of more expensive, complex, and age-worthy wines are made, but these are harder to find. Still crisp and fresh, they show more peach and pear fruit with an additional layer of chalk-like mineral complexity; and they can have higher alcohol and body. Punchy enough to pair with pesto-based dishes, risottos, some hard cheeses, and Mediterranean cuisine. Other Italian wines to try include Verdejo and Vermentino. Also try Sauvignon Blanc, Albariño, and Vinho Verde.

VINHO VERDE

A light, fresh wine made by the coast in northeast Portugal from a blend of local grape varieties. Dry and usually a pale lemony-green (though there are other styles and colors). This is ideal for summer sipping and as an aperitif. These lively wines are designed to be drunk young. Typically they have low alcohol, a tiny tongue-tingling *petillance*, or spritz, on opening, with fresh, young fruit, light flower hints, and an intense crispness. They are ideal for accompanying salads, a wide range of seafood, chicken, sushi, and gratins. Other wines to try include Vermentino, the more apple-y Chenin Blanc, a steely Chablis, more aromatic Sauvignon Blanc, and, for something with similar racy acidity, a Picpoul de Pinet.

Rosés

Column 9

40 G **Mt** Müller- Thurgau	**46** S **Wz** White Zinfandel

41 G **Po** Pinot Grigio	**47** G **Gb** Grenache	**52** R **Bj** Beaujolais
42 G **Al** Albariño	**48** R **Nv** Navarra	**53** G **Gm** Gamay
43 G **Pa** Parellada	**49** R **Ra** Rosé d'Anjou	**54** G **Do** Dolcetto
44 G **Ve** Verdicchio	**50** R **Pd** Pays d'Oc	**55** R **Va** Valpolicella
45 R **Vv** Vinho Verde	**51** R **Pc** Provence	**56** G **Bf** Blaufränkisch

The rosé wines appearing in this column are the more common styles obtainable; there are others, as many producers make a rosé alongside their other wines. These showcase the medley of rosé wines to sip, from off-dry and frivolous to serious, dry, and savory, including colors ranging from the palest of pretty pinks to the deepest of cherry-reds. Remember that a pale color does not always mean dainty flavors. Serve chilled to maintain their refreshing qualities.

Various red wines in the table are also made in a rosé style. These typically reflect the red-grape characteristics but are lighter, usually made without using oak. Frequently they are sold to be consumed while young, fresh, and fruity, though not always. If you like red wine, why not seek out the rosé to try and compare? Perhaps do so when the weather is a little too warm for red wine, although increasingly rosés are being drunk whatever the time of year. In the winter look for more warming, higher-alcohol versions, especially if they are well-made, with bold flavors and perhaps a slight texture to balance the alcohol.

WHITE ZINFANDEL

The name for a popular, soft, easy-drinking style of off-dry California rosé made from the red Zinfandel grape, but confusingly, the "white" in front of the grape variety means it is a rosé. It is also called "blush," which is less confusing. Here the Zinfandel grapes are picked early to retain freshness, which balances red-fruit flavors like strawberries, red currant, and watermelon. This early harvesting also ensures alcohol levels are lower: around 10 percent ABV. Their pretty pink color, gained from a short steeping of the grapes in the juice before fermentation begins, and lack of tannins combined with the fruit-juice style, make them popular for midweek drinking, despite the confusing nature of the name. A value-priced fresh and fruity wine made for drinking chilled, while it is still young. Unexpectedly, white Zin is a great match for spicy food such as Thai cuisine and curries, picnics, "sofa-sipping," and al fresco dining. This style is a good introduction to rosé for young palates as it is not as serious as some rosés. Also try other rosés, famously Mateus Rosé from Portugal, New World rosés, along with drier styles from the Rhône and Provence.

GRENACHE

Widespread leading red grape variety, used across the globe to make rosé wines in a range of colors, from pale to shocking pink, and in styles varying from cheeky and cheerful to sultry and serious. Alcohol levels can sometimes be high, especially where they are made in warmer climates, which allow the grapes to ripen well. Generally this diversity creates a variety of quality levels that is reflected in the price. Leaving the grape skins in contact with the fruity grape juice for different lengths of time affects the color of the wine. Popular lighter, fruity, less-alcoholic, wallet-friendly US styles are called "blush" and are similar to white Zinfandels. Also try picnic-friendly, deeper-pink Spanish Garnacha rosados, then the more serious, weighty, and warming southern French rosés in a range of delightful pinks, from pale blushing-powder (Provence) to the deeper colors of the southern Rhône. As alcohol levels can be high, they are not just summer aperitifs, but can work as autumn warmers as well. Grenache can be blended with other red grapes to bring red berry, cherry, and citrus flavors. The best have a touch of white pepper, cinnamon, and herbal notes. Serve chilled with salty snacks, cold meats, shrimp, and salmon. See Navarra and Provence, and compare with rosés from other areas, Bordeaux, Catalonia, and the New World.

NAVARRA

Important wine region in northern Spain, above Rioja along the Ebro River Valley, which is traditionally associated with large volumes of dark-pink rosado (rosé) wine from the Garnacha (Grenache) red grape variety. Rosados are usually dry, lush, and fruity, with flavors of soft strawberries and riper raspberries, sometimes a hint of rose, too. They are easy-drinking, with a fuller body and more alcohol—around 12 percent ABV—compared to white Zinfandel. Navarras are often pure Grenache, or Grenache blended with other red grapes like Spanish Tempranillo and international plummy Merlot. (As Navarra is located between France and Rioja, look out also for its accessible red and white wines, again from popular grapes like Tempranillo bolstered with other quality leading grape varieties.) Location combined with improvements in winemaking means there are now likeable wines from this region to please all tastes, occasions, and wallets. Good with tapas, salmon, and picnics. Try also velvety wines from neighboring Rioja, Rosé d'Anjou or lighter red wines such as Beaujolais, and Pinot Noir and Dolcetto, which are also available as rosés.

ROSÉ D'ANJOU

A style of rosé wine made in the Anjou region of France's Loire Valley from a blend of red grapes, including the local Grolleau, plus better-known Cabernet Franc and the Gamay grape used in Beaujolais wine. Often pale, peachy, and pomegranate-tinged, with a light to medium weight and low alcohol of around 10.5 percent ABV, these medium-dry, quaffable, salmon-colored wines are made for early drinking. Expect a fruity bouquet accompanied by classic rosé flavors of red berries, strawberries, and red currants, a touch of floral rose and confectionery, but with an uplifting freshness from good acidity and hints of mint, herbs, or white pepper. Serve chilled with savory dishes using gentle spices, or salmon or cold meats and light desserts such as fruit salads. Other wines to try are the dry Rosé de Loire, sweet Cabernet d'Anjou, and the more serious, rare Sancerre, made from Pinot Noir grapes. Compare with rosés from outside France: white Zinfandel or, with more alcohol, Spanish Riojas and Navarras.

PAYS D'OC

Pays d'Oc is a large appellation in southern France that makes all colors of affordable wine across the Languedoc. This classification is now known as Indication Géographique Protégée (IGP)—i.e., protected geographical indication—and it can be found on wines from defined large districts across Europe (as well as on foods such as cheddar and Parmigiano Reggiano cheeses). The dry rosés made in this Mediterranean location are often crafted from a blend of local red grapes. These can include rich Syrah and Cinsault, which add herbs and spiciness, along with soft, red-fruited, warming Grenache and deeper Mourvèdre. These rosés may have a touch of tannin from the skins that adds texture to balance the juiciness. Ripe, sunny, medium- to full-bodied with medium to high alcohol levels, these are best served chilled as an aperitif or as a partner for light dishes like herbed shrimp, tuna, and Mediterranean cuisine. Compare with rosados from Spain, or rosés from Sicily, cheerful northern Italian versions, and more specific southern French rosés like bone-dry Bandol.

51   R

Pc

Provence

PROVENCE

A hilly coastal Mediterranean region in the south of France that gives its name to attractive, often very pale, pink wines that can have *gris* ("gray") in their names. They are frequently fragrant or perfumed dry rosés made from a variety of different grapes, often as blends. Provence is the world's largest region to specialize in dry rosé, so it is not surprising that this area displays a wide range of colors and textures, with some wines being lighter and others fuller in body and flavors. Experiment in this area of wine. Expect soft red fruits plus herb, floral, and green fragrances redolent of the local *garrigue*: the name for the rosemary, lavender, and thyme that grow throughout the region. More full-bodied versions include pink-grapefruit notes balanced with a mineral, talc-like backbone and a hint of spice. The better wines can have a long, lingering flavor. Look for the special hourglass-shaped Provence rosé bottle called a skittle. The wines should be crisp, refreshing, food-friendly, and versatile: for example, the lower-alcohol (around 12 percent ABV) examples make ideal aperitifs. They are a good match with seafood, pork, chicken, salads, and of course Mediterranean dishes. Try also dry Tavel rosé for something more serious, and sweeter white Zinfandel for a more frivolous drink. Spanish Navarra rosés are usually darker pinks and, along with rosés from the New World, tend to be full of riper fruits like red plums, and are perhaps less floral in nature.

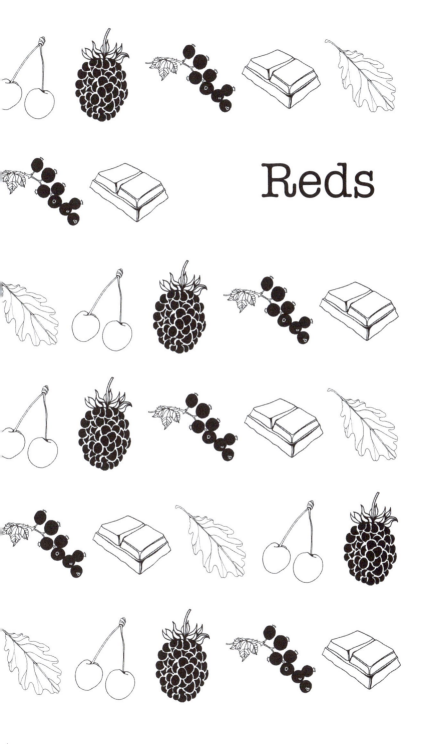

Reds

Column 10

		57 R **Ct** Chianti
46 S **Wz** White Zinfandel		58 G **Bb** Barbera
47 G **Gb** Grenache	52 R **Bj** Beaujolais	59 G **Pm** Pinot Meunier
48 R **Nv** Navarra	53 G **Gm** Gamay	60 R **By** Burgundy
49 R **Ra** Rosé d'Anjou	54 G **Do** Dolcetto	61 G **Pn** Pinot Noir
50 R **Pd** Pays d'Oc	55 R **Va** Valpolicella	62 G **Mp** Montepulciano
51 R **Pc** Provence	56 G **Bf** Blaufränkisch	63 R **Cn** Chinon

Light reds are a good place to start if you are unsure about red wine or you are after a lunchtime red for sipping alongside light meals. Typically made with less tannin, either due to the grape variety or winemaking techniques, they are really quaffable, and some are pleasant served just lightly cooled.

BEAUJOLAIS

Usually a light, fruity, easy-drinking red wine named after the region—south of Burgundy in France—where this juicy wine is made with Gamay grapes. Expect to find red fruits like strawberries, cherries, cranberries, and maybe pomegranates in your glass. Beaujolais can be pretty, full of flowery raspberries and violets plus sometimes hard-candy notes wrapped up with refreshing acidity. Most (but not all) Beaujolais wine is made to drink young. Historically it used to be about the race to be the first to try Beaujolais Nouveau, the "new" wine barely out of the barrel. Today, more finesse is found, especially in the better Beaujolais-Villages wines, and those at the best quality level, called *cru*. They have names on their labels like the prettily and aptly named floral Fleurie, or the more powerful and serious Brouilly and Morgan; others have slightly deeper flavors. One for the non-red-wine-drinkers to try, plus it can be served slightly chilled due to low tannin levels. A lovely, elegant wine to accompany informal lunches, pork, light roasts, and chicken casseroles or scrambled eggs. Try also Dolcetto or a light Pinot Noir.

GAMAY

This juicy red grape is light in tannins and tends to make typically light-bodied wines that are high in refreshing acidity and boast lively red-fruit flavors. The name of this grape variety might be unfamiliar, but it is the sole basis of the French Beaujolais (see above), plus a little is used in the Loire Valley farther west, and Gamay is also blended with the Pinot Noir grape to make the hard-to-find Dole in Switzerland. Gamay is usually made to be drunk young due to the production method that brings out the red-berry flavors and candied elements of strawberries in syrup, bubblegum, and bananas, so look out for recent vintages. There may also be a leafy green element. A small proportion of wines are being made in more robust styles, so are more like Pinot Noir, a little farther north in Burgundy. They have the ability to age. Gamay's light nature means it can be served slightly chilled so it's great with a summer picnic or platter of cold meats. Older—and pricier—wines are more serious and can taste like older wines made from Pinot Noir. This is a good "transition wine" for those who like white wines and want to try reds.

DOLCETTO

Dolcetto is a juicy red grape from the Piedmont region in northwest Italy. Its name means "little sweet one," although its wines are nearly always dry. Winemakers tend to use techniques to reduce tannins, happily resulting in easy-drinking, red-fruited wines typically made without oak, so these youthful sippers can be enjoyed soon after production. This grape makes soft-styled (softer than Barbera), less acidic, fruity, often intensely colored fragrant wines. Violets and even bitter almonds can accompany red cherry and summer dessert flavors. Occasionally fun, strawberry-laced sparkling wines are produced. Look for the Italian wines called Dogliani, Dolcetto d'Alba, and Dolcetto d'Acqui. Also try the firmer, more tannic Barbera from the same region, or Italian Valpolicella—both have a more acidic tang. Further afield, choose French Beaujolais or light Pinot Noirs. Perfect for antipasti, informal lunches, and buffets.

55	R
Va	
Valpolicella	

VALPOLICELLA

Valpolicella is a famous northeastern Italian district that makes a range of juicy red wines from a blend of local grapes. There is a ladder of quality levels. Most wine is the lightest, affordable, lunchtime-sipper style called Valpolicella *classico*. Next, *superiore* has more concentration and a touch more alcohol: around 12 percent ABV. *Ripasso* wines are made via a special technique to give a rich, but soft, medium-bodied wine. See Amarone for the full-bodied, big-fruited, and high-alcohol style. Valpolicella wines are fresh and elegant, with red-fruit flavors such as cherry and plum, plus herbs like thyme, as well as a slightly bitter finish that adds to the food-friendliness. Usually lighter alcohol, but not always, so check the label. Drink with snacks, pasta, and hard cheeses. Try also Beaujolais, Dolcetto, and Montepulciano.

BLAUFRÄNKISCH

A versatile red grape that makes wines ranging from deeply colored, ripe, earthy reds that can be graceful, light-bodied and fruity, to more intense, heavier-oaked, juicy, and denser examples. Mainly Austrian, but also used in Hungary and Eastern European countries, although the grape variety there could be labeled Lemberger or Kékfrankos. The versatility of this grape means more affordable, youthful, easy-drinking light styles are produced but still with a lush and velvety texture, blackberries and cherries, and a touch of elderflower and savory notes. Look for crisp, cherry flavors, sometimes a tannic backbone. The best, with big prices, are made from old vines or *alte Reben*, and so are fuller-bodied, with firm tannins: quite a different style and likely to see a bit of oak, so look on the label for information. Depending on how the wine is made, Blaufränkisch makes a fashionable alternative to many different grapes like Nebbiolo, Syrah, and Pinot Noir, therefore it is increasingly appearing on wine lists, together with its Austrian cousin Zweigelt. One to try if you come across it.

Column 11

		64 G **Pz** Pinot Noir: NZ
	57 R **Ct** Chianti	65 R **Ps** Pic St-Loup
	58 G **Bb** Barbera	66 G **M** Merlot
52 R **Bj** Beaujolais	59 G **Pm** Pinot Meunier	67 R **St** St-Émilion
53 G **Gm** Gamay	60 R **By** Burgundy	68 R **Rj** Rioja
54 G **Do** Dolcetto	61 G **Pn** Pinot Noir	69 G **Sg** Sangiovese
55 R **Va** Valpolicella	62 G **Mp** Montepulciano	70 G **Br** Brunello
56 G **Bf** Blaufränkisch	63 R **Cn** Chinon	71 G **Cm** Carmenère

Many red wines fit into the medium-bodied style, which is versatile and can include the most popular and well-known wines of the world—especially as they are frequently neither too tannic or heavy nor too light. This column starts with a large category of reds that continue into the next few columns. Their alcohol levels, as well as flavors and textures, are often mediums, although with such a big category and so many winemakers and places where they are made around the world, there is still a great deal of variation. Winemakers might make a selection of wines of different quality levels too.

57	R
Ct	
Chianti	

CHIANTI

A widespread region in Tuscany that makes popular juicy, ruby-red dry wines mainly from Sangiovese grapes, which are much improved since the rounded, raffia-clad, mass-produced *fiasco* bottles—although the latter are making a retro comeback. They come in a wide range of prices that generally reflect quality. Smoother, more refined Chiantis have *Classico* (the traditional heartland of Chianti) on the label, plus some other more specific regions, like the more floral Rúfina. *Riserva* wines have been aged for a minimum of two years before sale, which adds body, softness, and earthiness, while younger versions are juicy and fruity, with flavors of sour cherries (a classic Chianti tone), damson plums and wild herbs, smoke, and spice notes. Typical mellow tannins make them easy-drinking and well-liked. Premium-priced *gran selezione* Chiantis are rare, aged longer, and originate from single vineyards, offering more complexity, body, and lingering flavors. All usually have zippy acidity, which makes them excellent with a wide range of foods: antipasti (naturally), pasta and pizza, also medium cheeses, tomato-based dishes, and slow-cooked meats such as lamb and beef. Also check

out Sangiovese, good-value Rosso di Toscana, plus
Barbera, Vino Nobile di Montepulciano, Carmignano,
Merlot, and Rioja.

BARBERA

58   G
Bb
Barbera

The name of an Italian red grape variety that makes
succulent, medium- and some light-bodied, vivid,
easy-drinking, mostly Italian wines, with fleshy red fruits
such as cherries and raspberries, some with a touch of
smokiness or vanilla. This grape is local to northwest
Italy; think Barbera d'Asti ("Barbera from Asti") and
Barbera d'Alba ("Barbera from Alba"), with some
plantings in Argentina too. These wines can have light
or supple tannins (where a touch of oak is used, as the
grape itself is low-tannin) and a silky finish; refreshing
Italian acidity makes this a popular plummy wine. More
affordable in wines called *vino rosso*, where it could
be used as part of a blend. Great with mushroom- or
tomato-based pasta dishes like ravioli. Try also Merlot-
based wines, or from Italy, softer Dolcetto, Chianti,
or the lighter, herby Valpolicella. It is interesting to
compare with the very differently styled local but much
more tannic, serious, and pricey Barbaresco and Barolo
wines. Further afield, a juicy red-fruited Beaujolais from
France is a similarly styled alternative.

PINOT MEUNIER

59   G
Pm
Pinot
Meunier

Important red grape variety most famously used as
a partner with red Pinot Noir and white Chardonnay
grapes to make Champagne in northern France, and
also sparkling wines from other regions, although it
is a bit of a forgotten grape in the still-wine sector.
Meunier means "miller" in French, so-called because
the underside of the grape leaves appear to have
a dusting of flour. It can add a touch of patisserie,
apples, and sometimes a smoky note to Champagne
and her lookalikes. Proudly used by the prestige Krug

Champagne house. Krug aside, this grape is often used by more commercial Champagne and sparkling wine houses outside of France, so if you buy a wallet-friendly sparkling wine, you may be drinking Pinot Meunier without knowing it. Lighter in color and tannins than Pinot Noir, but with higher acidity, which adds freshness and is helpful when making bubbles.

BURGUNDY

Historic, influential French wine region that gives its name to red Pinot Noir and white Chardonnay dry wines. *Bourgogne* in French, it has variable weather, a patchwork of vineyards, and variety of soils; there is therefore a variety of quality in its wines. Confusingly, this is combined with the complicated classification system for wines made in Burgundy; it therefore becomes advisable to find a winemaker whose style you know you like. The classification system here categorizes wine quality by vineyard location. Uncomplicated *Bourgogne* (on the label) represents over half of production and grapes can come from anywhere in Burgundy. At the apex of this hierarchy are the exclusive, expensive *grand cru* wines from tiny single vineyards (named on the label in capital letters); these can age for decades. In between are district appellations such as Mâcon through to village names (communes in Burgundy) such as Puligny-Montrachet, up to single-vineyard communes, or *premiers crus*. Red burgundies are pale-colored, low-tannin, and light-bodied with violet hints and red fruits like red currants, raspberries, and cherries; they are also earth- and herb-scented. Aromas can be beguiling. Flavors can have an inner, graceful strength. They tend to have a chalklike mineral edge which, along with acidity, gives poise and elegance to these wines over those from outside Burgundy. The best keep developing to evolve savory, game, and mushroom layers with a silky texture, and the use of French oak barrels adds a subtle cream, vanilla, and smokiness (to both the red and white wines), but these wines can be high-priced. Pair them with roast chicken, herby pork or sausages, light game, dishes with morel mushrooms, and coq au vin. Other reds to try are fruitier Beaujolais, or go for a Pinot Noir from outside Burgundy, which may be riper.

PINOT NOIR

A light-colored, light-tannin, perfumed, leading red grape variety, usually not blended with other varieties. This fussy red grape is famously the aromatic red wine of the Burgundy region, its homeland. It reflects the different geological aspects, like soil, in which it is grown and is a style to which winemakers worldwide aspire. Pinot Noir can be complex, but is often more costly than other grape varieties, due in part to its small production and because it requires more work than other red grapes. Burgundian wines are dry and elegant, with poise, refreshing acidity, red cherries, and blackberries with violet perfume. With age, earthy, mushroomy undergrowth and gamy characteristics develop. Oak is used subtly in the winemaking process, adding a hint of cream—perhaps vanilla— and smokiness. Pinot Noir is a good match for food like pork, cold cuts, quiche, herby dishes, and light mushroom dishes.

From the New World, especially New Zealand and the United States, these red wines are much bigger, richer, deeper-colored, and riper, with darker cherries, damsons, and perhaps a touch of cooked fruit compote and leather on the palate—not always so aromatic, but perhaps more consistent. Quite a range of styles is produced in New Zealand alone, as experience and spread of the grape in the country grows. From cool-climate coastal Australian vineyards you can find pale-ruby Pinots with fruity flavors of raspberries. Wines from Chile are more straightforward. Pinot Noir from Oregon is a halfway-house style, somewhere between that of Burgundy and New Zealand. Alcohol is medium, body is medium, though both may be on the lighter side in Burgundy and heavier or riper outside the region. Refreshing acidity tends to be a touch more present in Pinot Noirs from Burgundy. Pairs well with baked sea bass, pheasant, herby leg of lamb, and vegetarian tarts.

MONTEPULCIANO

Montepulciano d'Abruzzo is a popular, juicy red wine made primarily from plummy Montepulciano grapes grown in the hilly Abruzzo region of central Italy. This is a deep-ruby, generally medium-bodied (some fuller-bodied examples are made), rounded wine, with lots of red cherries, plums, dried herbs, and supple tannins, so a little softer and less acidic than Chianti. It can include savory notes such as herbs, truffles, and pepper. Young wines can be more rustic and lighter, which makes them charming and versatile with food. Though a range of styles and prices is available, most are good-value, lighter, easy-drinking bottles of straightforward delicious dry red wine. *Riservas* are aged so are generally more complex—smoother, with layers of flavors like a touch of spice. Like many Italian wines, high acidity helps Montepulciano pair well with food, including tomato-based dishes, pasta, pizza, pulled pork, and hard cheeses. Try lighter, fruitier Valpolicella or Merlot, or go for something much deeper and sunnier like a Sicilian Nero d'Avola.

CHINON

A region in France's Loire Valley, named after its medieval fortress town, which also gives its name to dry red wines made predominantly with herby, aromatic Cabernet Franc grapes. (A tiny proportion of Chinon wines are cherry-fruited rosé and pale, crisp, quince-flavored whites made from Chenin Blanc grapes.) Here, year of production—the vintage—can be important. Chinons are light- to medium-bodied raspberry, summer pudding, fruity reds. They can have soft tannins or they can be more evident, with darker blueberry fruit, graphite hints of pencil shavings plus vanilla and tobacco-leaf notes as they are more likely to have seen a touch of oak. Cabernet Franc is more herby, with red and black fruits (*fruits de bois*) and fewer tannins and black currant compared with Cabernet Sauvignon. It can be a touch "green" in a cooler vintage, where the grapes have struggled to ripen. All Chinon wines have good levels of refreshing acidity and a suggestion of chalk minerals from the *tuffeau* ("freestone") soils, making them suitable to accompany picnic food and white meats, gently braised meats, charcuterie, buffets, and informal lunches. Look for names like Bourgueil and Saumur-Champigny made in neighboring villages. Also try slightly lighter Beaujolais, plummy Merlots, and richer Cabernet Francs from further afield, like Chile, which have a sunnier, riper, more viscous texture. Dolcetto, Barbaresco, Chianti, and young Rioja are good options for a change.

Column 12

	64 G **Pz** Pinot Noir: NZ	**72 R** **Rd** Ribero del Duero
57 R **Ct** Chianti	**65 R** **Ps** Pic St-Loup	**73 G** **Ma** Malbec
58 G **Bb** Barbera	**66 G** **M** Merlot	**74 R** **Cô** Côtes du Rhône
59 G **Pm** Pinot Meunier	**67 R** **St** St-Émilion	**75 G** **Te** Tempranillo
60 R **By** Burgundy	**68 R** **Rj** Rioja	**76 R** **Bs** Barbaresco
61 G **Pn** Pinot Noir	**69 G** **Sg** Sangiovese	**77 R** **Lg** Languedoc
62 G **Mp** Montepulciano	**70 G** **Br** Brunello	**78 G** **Pi** Pinotage
63 R **Cn** Chinon	**71 G** **Cm** Carmenère	**79 R** **Bx** Bordeaux

This column encompasses some of the world's most well-liked red wines and grape varieties, which makes the wines good for gatherings and everyday drinking. Sometimes they are made to age, which tends to be reflected in a higher price. This is an area of the table where you can experiment, moving up and down and between columns.

PINOT NOIR: NEW ZEALAND

New Zealand has achieved status for its own style of red wine made from Pinot Noir grapes (as it has for white Sauvignon Blanc). These wines are dry, with ripe red and black fruits, sunnier, and more concentrated than Old World Pinot Noir, but more elegant than the even riper, heavier Californian versions. A variety of styles is being produced as experience and vineyard locations grow. Typically wines are ripe, with flavors of dark plum and sometimes chocolate, cherry, and spicy notes from oak use. Medium-bodied, with soft tannins (higher than Burgundy). Look out for the alcohol level, which can be high, but it is balanced by the intense flavors. Older bottles have savory, herby, and earthy characteristics. New Zealand Pinot Noir is a versatile partner with food served with chutney or sauce trimmings, such as turkey, game birds and duck, roasted fillet of salmon, pork, veal, herby lamb, and venison. Compare this with a more subtle Burgundy, a bigger Californian Pinot Noir, and those from the New World. You might also like plummy Merlot, Chinon, and Rioja.

PIC ST-LOUP

A mountain close to the Mediterranean gives its name to this appellation within the Languedoc region of southern France. The appellation makes perfumed dry red wines from a blend of three main grapes: Syrah, Grenache, and Mourvèdre (a little rosé is also made).

These wines are ripe, which can give the impression of sweetness, with suggestions of *garrigue*: the rosemary, lavender, and thyme that grow across the region. There should be lots of fruit, plums, dark cherries, chocolate, and smoke, plus spicy notes of pepper from the Syrah and licorice. Sometimes there are savory olive flavors. Tannins can be rustic to silky, and body not less than medium, depending on the blend and the winemaker. Alcohol levels can be high, especially in the bigger, more intense wines, so check the label. Wines with more concentration and fuller body might be labeled *vieilles vignes* (made with grapes from old vines) and sell at a premium. Decanting will soften the wine before drinking. A great pair with barbecues, casseroles, ragoût, and herby lamb. Other wines from the area to try include Fitou, Corbières, Minervois, and wines from the more affordable Languedoc—the Pays d'Oc name.

MERLOT

A leading soft, plummy, red grape variety, which is popular with winemakers and wine-lovers all around the globe due to its easy-drinking nature and fruitiness. This is one of the main red grapes of Bordeaux wines, along with Cabernet Sauvignon, but Merlot is more velvety, with lower acidity and less tannin, so it can be approachable in youth. Better-value Bordeaux typically has a bigger proportion of Merlot within its blend. It is part of some of the world's most expensive wines and also wines that offer great value for money. Look for New World wines from Chile and Argentina, and less-well-known regions such as Fronsac and Languedoc-Roussillon for best value. This plump, mellow red, with its inclusive style, makes a good choice for a party, with flavors that include cherries, raspberries, and plums. Richer wines, often from warmer areas, are riper and more concentrated in style. Graphite, cedar, tobacco, smokiness, vanilla, and cloves may also be present,

66   G

M

Merlot

especially when oak is employed in the winemaking process. It can be made as a single-varietal wine—i.e., with only Merlot in the bottle—but just as often as part of a blend. Merlot's broad appeal is due in part to it pairing well with many foods, including stews and roasts, cheeses, and pâtés, but take care not to overwhelm it with strong flavors or spices. Other soft sippers include Rioja, Tempranillo, and, for a touch more warmth, a red Côtes du Rhône.

ST-ÉMILION

67	R
St	
St-Émilion	

St-Émilion is a pretty town in the Bordeaux region of France, on the right bank of the Gironde Estuary. Its name is associated with easy-drinking red wines. (The main wines of Bordeaux from the left bank of the estuary focus on Cabernet Sauvignon.) Here in this part of the Bordeaux region, these popular St-Émilion wines are based on softer, mellow Merlot, often blended with Cabernet Franc (and sometimes a splash of Cabernet Sauvignon). Wines are rounded, with red fruit—cherry, raspberry, plum—accompanied by a herbal note. Good overall balance and structure come from fresh acidity, and medium tannins, lower than Cabernet Sauvignon, make this red a crowd-pleaser. If oak is used, other layers of flavors such as vanilla, smoke, and spice add complexity. Some can be elegant and silky-smooth. A few winemakers are known for their more opulent and rich wine styles, but this comes at a price. Pair with roast meats and casseroles, herby veggie burgers, and sausages. Try the smooth, rich, black-cherryish, Merlot-based wines from neighboring Pomerol and the more affordable Lalande-de-Pomerol; also Merlots from around the world; the red grape Carmenère, which has a similar taste to Merlot; soft Rioja; the more sour-cherry-like Chianti, and higher-tannin Bordeaux reds. See Bordeaux and Médoc.

RIOJA

The most famous Spanish wine region is situated in northern Spain along the river Ebro, and is named after the river Oja, which flows into the Ebro near Haro. Rioja gives its name to mainly dry reds, plus a smaller amount of white and deeply colored rosé wines. Red wines range from soft and red-fruited, with no or little oak influence, to wines with plums, darker, richer, dried fruits, touches of leather, and sweet spices.

Mellow Riojas are released after aging, mainly in American oak, which adds coconut, vanilla, and spicy notes to the fruit and softens the tannins. With longer aging, like in the rarer *gran reserva* wines, the fruit turns to dried dates, along with earthy, mushroomy, savory, and leather characteristics that linger. Tempranillo, Garnacha, and a little Graciano form part of the Rioja grape blend. Garnacha dominates in the juicy, strawberry- and herb-filled dry rosés, called *rosados*, that can have higher alcohol levels than the sweeter and lighter US rosés.

White Riojas vary from modern, clean, fresh, easy-drinking styles to the traditional creamy, soft-fruited kinds that have been fermented in barrels; look for oak use on the label—it rounds out the flavors and texture. Oaked whites are suitable for more robust-styled meals, such as roast chicken and creamy sauces, pastas, and risottos, while the lighter styles are refreshing for summer food: salads, fish, and buffets.

Reds are food-friendly and crowd-pleasers, pairing well with lots of savory dishes: classically lamb, but also meat pies and less-delicate-tasting seafood—think paella. Compare the flavors of Riojas with their different classifications: *crianza*, *reserva*, and the premium *gran reserva*. You can also try wines from neighboring Navarra, Tempranillos, Merlots, and Montepulcianos.

SANGIOVESE

This is a widely planted and popular red grape in Italy, traditionally in Tuscany, where it is valued for its zippy acidity, sour cherry and herb tones, hints of tomato leaf, and the savory and earthy characteristics it gives to the red wines of Chianti. Some Chiantis bring out the floral characteristics of this grape more, like the violet notes in Chiantis from Rúfina. Sangiovese is also the only grape used to make Brunello di Montalcino and it is the majority grape of Vino Nobile di Montepulciano and Carmignano wines. Popular "Super Tuscan" wines pair Sangiovese effectively with international grape varieties such as Cabernet Sauvignon and Cabernet Franc, Merlot, and sometimes Syrah. In Corsica, where it is known as Nielluccio, expect to find more herb-like aromatics and flavors. A wide range of quality is available, so finding a good Sangiovese is confusing, especially as label names may look similar, although price is a good indication. Tannins are firm but not drying. Where the wine spends time in oak, a deeper plummy richness develops, along with earthy notes, plus leather. A natural choice for Italian dishes such as pasta and pizzas, Sangiovese is versatile, so in addition try it with ragu, charcuterie, bread and cheeses, and tomato-sauce based recipes.

BRUNELLO

Brunello is a red grape variety. It is the Sangiovese grape (of Chianti wine fame), but when grown in the region of Montalcino it is called a different name due to its deeper color. Brunello is often followed by *di Montalcino*—i.e., "Brunello from Montalcino." Montalcino is a hilltop town south of Siena in Tuscany where this type of Sangiovese is the sole grape used to make these aged, complex, dry wines with a full range of flavors. The wines are more forthright than Chiantis, and can be succulent, full of generous blackberry fruit, accompanied by herbal and menthol notes. These wines may also include a touch of savory earthiness, and will age further to give tannins a velvety softness. There is a range of prices, but Brunellos are not usually low-priced, and vintage variations exist. Decanting can help open up a wine before drinking. For a more wallet-friendly version, released after much shorter aging, try the fruitier, softer, and lighter Rosso di Montalcino, which is closer in style to Chianti. Compare with softer Chianti, more tannic Nebbiolo wines like Barolo, and smokier Pinotage. Brunello pairs with flavorful black olives and pine nuts, roasted meats, mushroom risotto, and savory herb dishes.

CARMENÈRE

This red grape variety is grown mainly in Chile as its signature grape. It originated in France in the Médoc region of Bordeaux, but more sun in Chile allows this gently herbaceous grape to shine. As a varietal wine it is fruity, with tones of dark blackberries, herbs, and spices, and boasts a dark color. It can have notes of black pepper and even tomato, or chocolate and cassis overtones when riper. Carmenère tends to have more herb and leaf notes compared to Merlot, and cedar where oak is used. With similar smooth, well-rounded tannins to those of Merlot, it is perhaps a touch lighter and more supple than Cabernet Sauvignon wines. It can come blended with these grapes or on its own. These easy-drinking red wines accompany meaty dishes, stews, pizzas, sausages, herby lamb chops, and nut cutlets. You might also like Cabernet Franc, Merlot, Cabernet Sauvignon, and Bordeaux blends.

Column 13

64 G **Pz** Pinot Noir: NZ	72 R **Rd** Ribero del Duero	80 R **Pt** Priorat
65 R **Ps** Pic St-Loup	73 G **Ma** Malbec	81 R **Bd** Bandol
66 G **M** Merlot	74 R **Cô** Côtes du Rhône	82 R **Cp** Châteauneuf- du-Pape
67 R **St** St-Émilion	75 G **Te** Tempranillo	83 G **Ci** Cinsault
68 R **Rj** Rioja	76 R **Bs** Barbaresco	84 G **Gr** Grenache
69 G **Sg** Sangiovese	77 R **Lg** Languedoc	85 G **Ne** Nebbiolo
70 G **Br** Brunello	78 G **Pi** Pinotage	86 G **Na** Nero d'Avola
71 G **Cm** Carmenère	79 R **Bx** Bordeaux	87 G **Cf** Cabernet Franc

Here we are gently moving toward red wines that generally have more weight about them, but are not necessarily full-bodied. Check out the level of alcohol, and also whether or not they are made using oak, which can add spices and texture. Older versions have had time to soften. Those made in warmer places contain riper fruit flavors. Once more, winemakers can make sets of wines from a wallet-friendly, more affordable version to small amounts of premium-quality-level reds, which will have been made using the best grapes and most care. These wines pair well with a wide range of dishes, making them a versatile choice.

RIBERO DEL DUERO

A high-altitude region in Spain that makes deep-flavored, dark-colored, fine, dry red wines, mainly using Tempranillo grapes (called Tinto Fino here), with other grapes like Cabernet Sauvignon and Merlot forming part of the blends. Riberos are complex, with cherry fruit, licorice, and spices and supple, velvety-to-firm tannins plus alcohol, which can be high. They can have a touch of tobacco and can be rich and meaty, with chocolate tones and a fuller-bodied texture; the more powerful wines have higher prices to match, plus are more likely to have been aged in oak. Both American and French oaks are used, adding coconut, subtle vanilla, cream, and cedar layers of aromas and flavors. The oak-aging classification system here is the same as in Rioja (but without white wines). Decant into a new bottle if you prefer to aerate and soften the wine before serving. This welcoming red wine pairs well with goulash, tagines, and warming winter dishes such as shepherd's pie. Other hearty wines to try include lighter Riojas, plus with more of a black currant edge, Cabernet Sauvignon, ripe southern Rhône and Portuguese reds, and New World wines made from Grenache and Syrah.

MALBEC

A red grape variety grown fairly widely but mainly in Argentina, where it is the country's signature red wine. Historically it originates from Cahors, in southwest France. It makes popular dry wines that are ink-colored and can at times be full-bodied. It brings juicy fruit flavors ranging from blueberries (a classic note), black cherries, plums, and blackberries to the glass. Malbec is available in a range of weights (feeling plump in the mouth), with some wines more full-bodied than others, so find your own preferred style, perhaps depending on the occasion. Malbec grapes respond to differences in climate and soils. From Argentina, Malbec wines can have more blueberry than plum flavors, and some include a touch of violets—plus, they have higher levels of tannins than Merlot. They can be more rustic than Merlots too, and easier-drinking than Cabernet Sauvignons, especially the more affordable, lighter-styled versions, which are good for a party. Argentinian Malbecs are riper and sunnier, with a silky, more velvety texture compared to those from cooler Cahors. For French Malbecs, look for Cahors or Côt. These can be more savory than Argentinian versions, with firmer tannins—some very tannic, some more rustic—and with a touch of smokiness. Aging in oak softens tannins on both sides of the Atlantic, making the wines feel rounder in the mouth, and it can add flavors of figs, leather, and tobacco, plus spices like cloves and pepper. Sometimes Malbec is blended with other red grapes such as Cabernet Sauvignon or Merlot, reflecting its links with blended Bordeaux wines and adding flavor layers plus color. If you find it a little tough, decant it to soften and round it out. Try it with calves' liver, casseroles, steak, ragu, and mature cheeses. Surprisingly, a glass of juicy New World Malbec pairs well with a piece of chocolate cake. Other wines to try include Bordeaux, Côtes du Rhône, heavier and deeper Priorat, and Ribero del Duero.

CÔTES DU RHÔNE

A collective name for southern French wines made alongside the river Rhône. Côtes du Rhône covers the majority of wine made across the Rhône region, especially in those appellations close to the southern part of the Rhône River. Côtes du Rhône-Village is one up the quality ladder, so expect to pay a little more and find a touch more complexity of flavors, plus more assurance compared to standard Côtes du Rhône. Usually these popular wines are a blend of Grenache, Syrah, and Mourvèdre red grapes, with blending taking place at the bottling stage. Depending on how they are made, these juicy, warming, dry, sunny wines range from easy-drinking, medium-bodied, fruity, lighter tannin-styled reds to more pricey, fuller-bodied wines that bring increased levels of red and black fruits and peppery spiciness, plus tannins that soften with time to yield earthy, smoky, darker tones. (A small amount of usually fuller-bodied and well-rounded white and rosé Côtes du Rhône is made and is certainly worth trying.) This category of wine is recommended, as it is a versatile style for food- and friend-pairing, good for parties and also your wallet. Check the label for alcohol levels, which can be high. Try with pizza, pasta, buffets, shepherd's pie, and lasagna. You might also like Chianti, Rioja, and fuller-bodied Châteauneuf-du-Pape, which is also from the Rhône and a step up in quality. For much lighter wines, look toward Beaujolais and Dolcetto.

TEMPRANILLO

A red grape variety used to make medium- to full-bodied wines, especially from Spain: the mainstay of popular Rioja and the slightly sharper Ribero del Duero. Also used to good effect in wines from many other areas in Spain. In Portugal, where is it known as Tinta Roriz or Aragonês, it is used for both still, dry table wines and fortified Port. Wines are usually well-colored with a range of flavors, depending on where the grapes are grown and how the wine is made. Flavors change depending on regional climate and range from red fruits such as strawberries and raspberries, with herby and dusty notes in relatively cooler vineyards, but darker fruits like cherries, blackberries, plums, or prunes emerge if the grapes are grown in a hotter area. When Tempranillos are aged, expect earthy, mushroomy, and savory flavors with a pleasant finish. Alcohol levels vary, so look at the label. Tannins tend to be moderate. Except for the fruity, uncomplicated *vin joven* ("young wine") made for immediate drinking, wines are made with oak. A layer of vanilla and coconut aromas and flavors develop from the traditional use of American, rather than French, oak. Modern-styled Tempranillo uses more subtle French oak, which adds cream notes, rounding out the texture. Young, affordable wines are easy-drinking, with red fruits like cherries and plums, plus herbs and medium acidity levels, so these are great for gatherings, pizzas, lamb (a classic combo), and pasta. Leather, clove, and savory notes are found in the pricier, aged bottles, which suit herby, slow-cooked dishes with mushrooms. Location affects the grape and hence the style of wine, so Tempranillo has many synonyms depending on where it is grown, but this can be confusing; look for Tinto Fino in the Ribero del Duero wines, beefy dark Tinto de Toro and Cencibel. Try also Côtes du Rhône, Chianti, Merlot, and St-Émilion.

BARBARESCO

A province and wine appellation in Piedmont, northwest Italy, which gives its name to dry red wines made using just Nebbiolo grapes. Drinkable earlier, lighter, and less tannic compared to its big-brother neighbor, Barolo, these pale-colored, medium- to full-bodied wines are, like Barolo, fruity and floral when young, turning more savory when older, and can have high alcohol. With the characteristic Italian zip of fresh acidity, Barbarescos can be more elegant than Barolo, but are still rich and spicy with a suggestion of dried rose perfume combined with red berry– and raspberry-like fruit and perhaps a touch of earthiness—like the aromas released by digging with a shovel in damp ground. Like many Piedmont wines, this red goes well with mushrooms, especially truffle-infused dishes, stronger cheeses, game, and hearty casseroles. A more affordable alternative is Langhe Nebbiolo from the same region; plus, try other less tannic Italian wines, including Barbera, Chianti, and, to contrast, the fruity Valpolicella.

LANGUEDOC

This is a large, ancient, warm winemaking region in the south of France. It borders the Mediterranean, like Roussillon, its neighbor. Often their names are combined. Once known for volume, investment and improvements in all aspects of production have significantly improved quality, especially where vineyards combine sunshine for easy ripening with cooling sea breezes, or when planting occurs on the local mountainsides, which gives freshness to the grapes grown at altitude. A wide range of grapes thrives here, and many styles of wines are produced. Still, the Languedoc is predominantly a red wine region, producing wines that are rich, ripe, flavorsome, and often hearty, making use of blends of grapes like Syrah, Grenache, Carignan, and Mourvèdre. Also there is great experimentation with zingy to full-bodied whites. Sparkling wines called *crémants*, like Crémant de Limoux, offer a good-value alternative to Champagne, and importantly, the overlooked red and white fortified wines from this region make a fine accompaniment to the final course of a meal. This area's wines compete on the world stage, not only with other French wines but also with popular wines from the New World. Helpfully this region is permitted to include grape varieties on its wine labels. Whatever the style, generally there is value to be found in the Languedoc, so look here for alternatives to the pricier, more famous wine regions. The red wines pair well with cassoulet and Mediterranean cuisine.

PINOTAGE

78	G
Pi	
Pinotage	

South Africa's trademark versatile red grape is a twentieth-century crossing of Pinot Noir and Cinsault. Recent understanding of how best to treat it has improved the reputation and reliability of the smoky, mainly black fruit–filled wines made from it. Also expect licorice and sometimes savory flavors, as well as a suggestion of smoke or tar, not too much acidity, and reasonable tannin levels. Pinotage can come in a range of weights, depending on how the winemaker produces it. Youthful versions are lighter, with a touch more red fruit (raspberries); being softer, these wines are designed for early and easy drinking and are also easier on the purse. Jammier forms are available, with riper, cooked-fruit flavors. Some are all coffee and chocolate layers, which will typically be mentioned on the label. Premium versions cost more, show depth, and spend time in oak, which adds sweeter spices to the smoky tones and concentration. With heavier and more serious wines, decanting will lighten and aerate them for serving. This style can be aged (look for "bush vine" or "old vines" on the label). Occasionally Pinotage is made into distinctive rosé and sparkling wines. It is often mixed with other red grapes like the Cabernet Sauvignon and Merlot as a "Cape Blend," and with other varieties such as Shiraz and Cinsault. A go-to barbecue red, and also good with smoked foods, sausages, and ham. Find the style you like and also try Bordeaux "Cape Blends," or Carmenère, Shiraz, and GSM (Grenache, Syrah, and Mourvèdre blends).

BORDEAUX

Bordeaux is a vast wine region in southwest France along either side of the Gironde Estuary, and it is also the catchall appellation of mainly dry red wines, including the most famous wines in the world. (Dry whites are made from Sauvignon Blanc and Sémillon, from young, grassy, light, Entre-deux-Mers wines to rich and creamy, more of an oily-textured, oak-aged whites from the Pessac-Léognan region. Sweet wines are also made in Bordeaux; see Sauternes.) Here is an area where the year the wine is made, the vintage, can be important because variations in the climate each year affect how well the grapes ripen and which variety ripens best. In the UK, Bordeaux reds are also known as clarets, and are generally blends of Merlot and Cabernet Sauvignon, with splashes of Cabernet Franc and Petit Verdot thrown in for seasoning. There are different styles and prices due to the great number of producers and the huge volume of wine made in this large region. The better wines can age well and sell at premium prices. They are made using French oak. Look out for notes of cedar and cigar box. They should have a fine acidity, a mix of red and black fruits, no overripeness, with a classic Bordeaux nose and flavors of herbs, as well as suggestions of graphite and pencil-like mineral notes and sometimes smokiness from the oak. Where Cabernet Sauvignon dominates, more black fruit and tannins accompany the herbs (see Médoc), and these wines are more likely to need decanting to soften them for drinking. Where Merlot leads, the wine is more approachable, with plum and cherry tones and softer in style; see St-Émilion. Bordeaux wines are food wines; there is pretty much a Bordeaux available to accompany most dishes. Wines are made all over the globe with these same grapes, often known as a "Bordeaux blend," and should be readily available, with Chilean examples offering good value.

Column 14

72 R **Rd** Ribero del Duero	**80** R **Pt** Priorat	**88** G **Cs** Cabernet Sauvignon
73 G **Ma** Malbec	**81** R **Bd** Bandol	**89** G **Sy** Syrah
74 R **Cô** Côtes du Rhône	**82** R **Cp** Châteauneuf-du-Pape	**90** R **Ce** Côte-Rôtie
75 G **Te** Tempranillo	**83** G **Ci** Cinsault	**91** G **Du** Durif
76 R **Bs** Barbaresco	**84** G **Gr** Grenache	**92** R **Ba** Barolo
77 R **Lg** Languedoc	**85** G **Ne** Nebbiolo	**93** G **Mv** Mourvèdre
78 G **Pi** Pinotage	**86** G **Na** Nero d'Avola	**94** R **Ca** Cahors
79 R **Bx** Bordeaux	**87** G **Cf** Cabernet Franc	**95** R **Mé** Médoc

Red wines become richer and even more characterful here. This is perhaps not an area in which to start your red wine drinking. Bold flavors can be accompanied by high alcohol levels, so look at the label; some wines have grippier tannin concentrations too.

PRIORAT

A region in northeast Spain that gives its name to rich, juicy, intense, full-bodied red wines made from a blend of grapes that gives the wines an extensive range of flavors. Varieties used include earthy Carignan and generous strawberry Grenache augmented with peppery Syrah, Cabernet Sauvignon, and plummy, softer Merlot. Look for warm, ripe fruit, summer berries, sweet baking spices, and savory notes of tapenade. These generous, Mediterranean wines are still refreshing and can have significant herbal and mineral notes, depending on the soils in the vineyard, so could readily be at the bottom of the column. A combination of US and French oak is often used for aging. Wine that spends the least time in oak is most fruity, but long aging leads to more dried fruit and leather flavors evolving over time. Tannins vary from silky and integrated to firm with grip; here, decanting before drinking can aerate the wine, softening it and bringing out more flavors. Alcohol levels tend to be high, but this is matched by the flavors. Priorat wines pair well with nourishing food like steak-and-kidney pudding and shepherd's pie. Other hearty wines to sip include Châteauneuf-du-Pape, similar blends from Australia, and more affordable wines from the Languedoc, as well as lighter Côtes du Rhônes and wines from nearby Monsant.

BANDOL

A small seaside fishing village in Provence, Mediterranean France, famous for the spicy, powerful, dry red wines produced around the region. (Similarly styled rosés are made too, along with a tiny amount of whites.) Reds are robust and juicy, with firm tannins and high alcohol levels. They are made by blending hand-harvested grapes, primarily Mourvèdre, with generous Grenache—which adds a riper, red, fruity touch, and lower tannins—perfumed Cinsault, and cinnamon-spiced Syrah. Look for black currant and morello cherry in these sunny wines, along with a flash of Provençal herbs such as rosemary, thyme, and lavender. They are fruitier when young and can be kept too, with a few being extremely age-worthy. Sometimes nutty hummus and vanilla hints develop with time. A spicy savoriness and leather tones evolve with age. Bandols make a wonderful accompaniment to herby sausages, casseroles, and lasagna. Try wines from across the region since proximity to the sea and altitude, as well as the blend used, all impact on the flavor and structure of these mouth-filling wines. If you like this style, try more affordable Fitou and Corbières or splurge on a Châteauneuf-du-Pape, or one of its neighbors, Gigondas.

CHÂTEAUNEUF-DU-PAPE

An important village in the southern Rhône that gives its name to probably the most famous dry red wines of the region, which can be ripe, rich, powerful, and alcoholic. Châteauneuf can be made from a blend of up to thirteen different grape varieties, often with a large amount of fruity Grenache, along with spicy Syrah and more savory Mourvèdre. (A very small amount of rich, exotic, fruity and creamy white wines is made, but no rosé.) These popular wines are juicy, and can be jammy, with red and black fruit flavors, spiciness, and a touch of smokiness. They often show savory-sweet bouquets, with flowers and cinnamon accompanied by the thyme and rosemary that prevail in the area. Tannins tend to be ripe, due to the sunny Mediterranean climate. With age, they become more savory, almost brooding, and meaty. They can be pricey. Plenty is made; sometimes the cheaper wines do not necessarily live up to this appellation's hearty reputation. For a similar but more affordable style, try better-value wines from neighboring appellations like Vacqueras, Lirac, Rasteau or Côtes du Rhône-Villages. An Aussie GSM (Grenache, Syrah and Mourvèdre blend) made with comparable grapes can be riper and jammier, with even more cooked fruit compote. You might also like Amarone and Ripasso della Valpolicella. Châteauneuf is a great accompaniment to Thanksgiving dinner, hearty meals in the cooler months, and big cheeses.

CINSAULT

An ancient red grape variety that prefers heat, Cinsault is popular in the Mediterranean, where it is sometimes spelled without the "l." As a red wine it is usually a small part of a blend, so you are less likely to come across a red varietal Cinsault, but it can be found alone in its elegant and refreshing rosé incarnations, which are full of wild strawberry and juicy raspberry flavors. Cinsault is used a lot in the southern Rhône blends, adding softness (it is low in drying tannins), perfume, and more red berry flavors to Grenache, spicy Syrah, and/or the more savory, gamy Mourvèdre. It is permitted in Châteauneuf-du-Pape and neighboring wines, and is also found in the deeply colored, warming, spicy, and fruity wines of Languedoc-Roussillon, like Minervois and Corbières. It adds red fruit as part of South African wines, as well as to wines from Morocco, Lebanon, the United States, and Chile. As a single varietal its low tannins mean it is ideal for light, aromatic, and fruity rosés from Provence and surrounding regions.

See also Pinotage. And try Grenache. As a red or rosé, Cinsault complements dishes with spicy flavors, such as Moroccan-style lamb dishes, spicy roasted salmon, and aromatic rice.

GRENACHE

84   G
Gr
Grenache

A leading red wine grape variety, Grenache, or Grenache Noir, is used for making usually juicy, strawberry-filled, popular high-alcohol wines in a variety of styles and prices. (Less common are white Grenache Blanc grapes.) It is planted widely around the warmer, sunnier areas of the world, so can have high alcohol levels. It is known as Garnacha in Spain and Cannonau in Sardinia. An important component of many ripe, fruity southern French wines which are often blends, most famously Châteauneuf-du-Pape. For value, look to the Languedoc and Roussillon in France. Some of the French Grenache wines have a touch of the perfumed rosemary, thyme, and lavender *garrigue* about them, reflecting the greenery in this dry area. It is included in some Spanish Riojas and Navarra wines, where it is usually blended with the Tempranillo grape as it softens the resulting wine. More recently it has become an important element in dry, red, deep Priorat wines, also from Spain. Grenache is often mixed with other grapes, especially Syrah and Mourvèdre. In Australia, a deep, full-bodied, sunny, ripe "GSM" is a Grenache/Syrah/Mourvèdre blend; the Old Grenache vines make a more bold, concentrated, complex style of wine with lingering flavors, which is reflected in the price. Such a versatile grape (see also the Grenache rosé entry)—look out for sweet *vin doux naturel* wines from Banyuls and Maury in southern France, which are delicious with chocolate desserts.

NEBBIOLO

An old Italian red grape variety from the Piedmont region, Nebbiolo forms the basis of Barolo and Barbaresco wines, and, further afield, the more affordable Langhe wines. Named after the *nebbia*, or "fogs," of the region, this grape creates pale but intense, full-bodied, dry red wines where fresh acidity combines with flavors of dried cherries, mulberries, spice, and roses when young, but with age, savory layers of tea, tar, and earthiness emerge.

Depending on where it is grown, the minimum aging requirements for Nebbiolo change. Look for words like "*riserva*," which means the wines have been aged for longer. This extra time and work is reflected in their higher prices. When young, strong, drying tannins mean this red needs to accompany food. You can try decanting to make it more approachable as well as accentuating its truffle, licorice, and forest-floor aromas. With time, Nebbiolo's pale color turns brick-orange. It is used in other Italian wines that tend to be more affordable, like Roero, Ghemme, and Gattinara. Confusingly, the Nebbiolo grape is also known as Spanna and Chiavennasca. Similar wines to try include (without the tannin) a pale-colored aged Pinot Noir, or try Greek Xinomavro or older Riojas. This wine suits autumn and winter dining as its big, earthy tones pair with flavorful food such as thick stews, mushroom dishes, and stinky mature cheeses.

NERO D'AVOLA

An iconic and increasingly popular Sicilian red grape, sometimes called Calabrese. It is planted across the island, not only in Avola. In the past, its dark color meant it was used to bolster other grapes. Today it is much more likely to be the sole grape variety in medium- to full-bodied dry, fruity, and sometimes high-alcohol wines. Good winemakers create flavors and scents of violet and herbs, plums, cherries, raspberries, and some examples with peppery spices, rather than being too confected. Acidity is medium to refreshing. High, ripe tannins are often velvety, but decanting will soften those that are not so smooth. Those that use oak add toasted almond and vanilla hints. Look for wines from grapes grown on calcareous soil, which have a chalky thread of minerality running through the aromas and flavors. Try also Syrah, softer Merlot, and sunny wines from the Languedoc. Pairs well with lamb couscous, a tomato-beef casserole, and, of course, Mediterranean cuisine.

CABERNET FRANC

A red grape variety similar to Cabernet Sauvignon, this is its offspring (its other parent was Sauvignon Blanc), although often with less color and less tannin, making it softer, slightly more crisp, and more perfumed—a halfway point between Merlot and Cabernet Sauvignon. Found mostly as part of a blend, famously in Bordeaux, it also goes solo in the cooler Loire Valley in appellations like Chinon, Bourgueil, and Saumur. Here the greener, herby notes are noticeable, accompanied by a savory perfume of pencil shavings, plus a graphite-like minerality, tobacco where oak is used, blackberries, and black currant including the leaves. Grown widely across the world, but not at the same volumes as Cabernet Sauvignon and Merlot. In warmer locations Cabernet Franc has greater richness, as it is riper, with dark-plum notes, more sweet spices, and red licorice. Pairs well with hams, cassoulet, and pork chops. As well as Cabernet Sauvignon and Merlot, you might also like Syrah, Rioja, and Carmenère.

Column 15

		96 R **Am** Amarone
80 R **Pt** Priorat	**88** G **Cs** Cabernet Sauvignon	**97** G **Cg** Carignan
81 R **Bd** Bandol	**89** G **Sy** Syrah	**98** G **Sh** Shiraz
82 R **Cp** Châteauneuf- du-Pape	**90** R **Ce** Côte-Rôtie	**99** G **Zi** Zinfandel
83 G **Ci** Cinsault	**91** G **Du** Durif	**100** G **Pr** Primitivo
84 G **Gr** Grenache	**92** R **Ba** Barolo	**101** G **Pv** Petit Verdot
85 G **Ne** Nebbiolo	**93** G **Mv** Mourvèdre	**102** G **Ag** Aglianico
86 G **Na** Nero d'Avola	**94** R **Ca** Cahors	**103** G **Ng** Negroamaro
87 G **Cf** Cabernet Franc	**95** R **Mé** Médoc	**104** G **Ta** Tannat

Wines are moving into the full-bodied, bold reds here, with weight and textures in the mouth and often generous levels of tannins, which give these reds greater presence—if the grapes are not ripe enough at harvest, however, the tannins can be drying in the wine. These characteristics come from both the grape and the techniques used by the winemaker. These reds are usually darker in color because of the pigments in the grape skins, although Nebbiolo is famously paler. Expect to find darker, deep, red fruit flavors such as blackberries instead of raspberries. They may need time to soften, or try decanting them before serving. These forthright characteristics make this style of wine a good accompaniment to protein-rich foods like hearty meats and cheeses, as they soften and meld together.

CABERNET SAUVIGNON

"Cab Sauv" is a leading international and popular red grape variety planted all over the globe. Prices range from affordable to investment. It can be made as a single-varietal wine but is versatile enough to blend with many other varieties, which helps to balance the resulting wine. Fruity and savory, deep red, tannic, often black currant– or cassis-laden, much wine made from this grape is inspired by quality Bordeaux and often produced using French oak, which adds sweet spices and light vanilla tones and softens the texture. Frequently blended with Merlot and Cabernet Franc, or with Sangiovese in Italy's "Super Tuscans," it is also used as part of a blend in Spanish Priorat wines, as well as being a big wine on its own, superbly in Chile. Cabernet Sauvignon is a big, full-bodied wine. Younger wines and those from cooler regions are more blackberryish, with a herbal earthiness and notes of green pepper, tobacco, and licorice. You may prefer the wine after decanting softens it. Warmer regions give riper, fruitier wines, still with licorice and juicy dark cherries, dark plums, vanilla, and dark spices, sometimes with a menthol or eucalyptus note. Tannins are a little softer too. Alternatives include the mellower Merlot, Italian Nero d'Avola, Portuguese Touriga Nacional, and Malbec, plus for something deep-colored and more brooding, look to Syrah, Italian Aglianico, tricky-to-find Lagrein, Spanish Monastrell, and also Carmenère. Match with hearty winter meals, steaks, burgers, mushroom stroganoff, and braised beef.

SYRAH

A leading international and popular red grape variety, called Shiraz where it is grown in warmer regions, which tend to be in the New World (Chile, Argentina, Australia), since the style of the wine changes with climate. See also Shiraz. Syrah is deeply colored, usually full-bodied, and packed with dark fruit flavors. Age adds black pepper, black olive, herb, licorice, and sometimes savory bacon notes. Refreshing acidity imparts finesse and can be found in wines made in the cooler regions, plus it benefits the wine by making it more food-friendly. Depending on how the wine is made and its age, tannins can be medium to high. Higher-priced bottles can age. As a single-varietal wine, look for Crozes-Hermitage, St-Joseph, or Cornas, all from the northern Rhône, where black fruits and spices mingle. Southern Rhône wines include warming Syrah as part of a blend and can be high in alcohol, with the spices being a little softer than black pepper. Look out for Côtes du Rhône, and further south in France for competitively priced early-drinking wines that might mix Syrah with Grenache and Mourvèdre plus other punchy red grapes. These wines show elements of the herby *garrigue*—rosemary, thyme, and lavender—from the location. American winemakers called "Rhône Rangers" use Syrah in their wines that emulate the French versions, most of which are consumed in the United States. Try also Cabernet Sauvignon, Primitivo, and Durif. Syrah is a good accompaniment to bold dishes, including steaks, blue cheeses, and barbecue.

CÔTE-RÔTIE

The name of an ancient region in the north of France's Rhône Valley, after which its premium dry red wines made using spicy Syrah grapes are titled. The grapes are grown on steep slopes in vineyards overlooking the river Rhône. A splash of white Viognier grapes is permitted under the local winemaking rules. This adds a delicate perfume, like floral violet notes, and helps keep the deep color. A hearty full- to medium-bodied wine with complex flavors of summer, Côte-Rôtie offers black fruits like cherries and blackberries, along with sweet and black pepper spices and good levels of fine, silky tannins. Premium versions combine robustness with elegance from the wine's acidity. With age, woodland, leather, tobacco, and coffee notes can develop among the herbs. Syrah and Shiraz from Chile and Australia are riper, while Cabernet Sauvignon has more cassis and drier tannins, and Merlot is softer and plummier. Côte-Rôtie is a match for big dishes like beef daube, tapenade, beef ribs, and deeply flavored, spicy, mushroom-based vegetarian dishes.

DURIF

A deeply colored, originally French red wine grape, called Petite Sirah in California, where it prospers today. Durif also makes successful, concentrated, spicy, dark-fruited wines in Australia, often with chocolate, black pepper, and blackberry flavors. It is related to the Syrah wine grape and has similarities, although it is more straightforward in style. It, too, is full-bodied, inky, and rich, and has the potential to soften with age. "Petite" describes the size of the grapes. It has high levels of acidity—useful to keep it fresh, especially where it is grown in hotter regions. High levels of tannin make it a robust wine. Try it blended with Zinfandel and Shiraz, plus other full-bodied reds, including with more black-currant-y Cabernet Sauvignon, and the earthier Carignan, Mourvèdre, and Primitivo. For big foods like beef, dark mushroom dishes, and richly flavored curries.

BAROLO

A hillside village in Piedmont after which the pale, dry, powerful red wines made in the region solely from the local Nebbiolo grape are named. These are not wines for beginner red-wine drinkers because they are tannic and acidic in youth, requiring age to release the truffle plus mushroom notes, as well as always commanding high prices. Don't let their muted color fool you; they are powerful and full-bodied, can have high alcohol, and are famous for scents of tar or tea and roses. Old and new styles of winemaking collide here in northwest Italy. Modern styles use French oak to soften the tannins at a younger age, making them ready to drink earlier and retaining more of their strawberry fruit. Traditional styles are made by letting the juice and grape skins stay in contact for longer to extract more from the skins, so are less fruity and require more aging. Both styles benefit from decanting to soften the tannic structure, so allow the wine to spend some time with air in another bottle or decanter before drinking. Find a winemaker whose style you like, as the grape reflects the vineyard soil and general *terroir* as well as winemaking techniques used. The weather during the year, or vintage, affects the quality of Barolo wines, so experiment here too. Due to the characteristics of the Nebbiolo grape, minimum aging is legally required for the wines produced from it, to allow all the mulberries, violets, and spices to gather and transform with truffle and licorice, sometimes chocolate, complexity; check out older vintages, which might say "*riserva*" on the label. You could try more affordable neighboring

Barbaresco or simply a Nebbiolo from the Langhe region. Definitely a wine that needs food, otherwise the tannins can dry out your mouth. Great with osso buco and with mushroom- and truffle-based dishes.

MOURVÈDRE

A dark-skinned, usually high-alcohol, high-tannin red grape, similar to Cabernet Sauvignon but more rustic in style. It is called Monastrell in Spain, which has the largest area planted, where you could see "Jumilla" or "Yecla" on the label; here it is more gamy. It's also grown in France close to the Mediterranean and in the Rhône, as it likes heat. Often it is part of a blend, for instance with generous Grenache and cinnamon-spiced Syrah in the Rhône, and is key in the red wines from Bandol. Mourvèdre is full of earthy dark fruits, herbs, and spicy black pepper. For alternatives, try Malbec, Rhône blends, Cabernet Sauvignon, heavier Aglianico, spicier Shiraz, or Syrah, more tannic Cahors and Tannat, as well as juicy southern French Minervois, Corbières, and Fitou. This full-bodied (sometimes smoky, if oak has been used) red benefits from decanting and can stand up to big, protein-rich foods, like steak with black pepper sauce, mushrooms with Madeira, and savory umami dishes with plenty of Parmesan cheese. These rich, dark, earthy flavors soften the tannins. It is also used to great effect in rich, sweet, fortified wines such as Bandol that pair well with rich chocolate and dried fruit desserts, as well as dark fruit cakes.

CAHORS

A small French town east of Bordeaux that is the original home of deeply colored, full-bodied, dry red wines made mostly from the Malbec grape. These inky wines were traditionally known as the "black wines from Cahors." With flavors and aromas of black fruits plus earthy, damp-forest-floor characteristics, they tend to be more savory, with meat, plum, and blackberry notes, firmer tannins, and crisper acidity than the riper, more generous, blueberry-laden, creamier Mendoza Malbecs from Argentina. There are different styles made within the Cahors region, ranging from affordable, more straightforward, fruitier "traditional" wines to aged, more powerful, complex, and concentrated offerings, with prices to match as this style involves using oak, which adds clove, vanilla, and mocha notes. Look for the intense and complex *spéciale* wines and consider decanting to soften them and bring out more flavors before drinking. The Malbec grapes can be blended with small amounts of Tannat and plummier Merlot. Match this robust wine with similar food, like a hearty beef stew, game, or cassoulet as part of a rustic menu. As well as comparing Cahors with Argentinean Malbecs, other wines to try include cassis-laden Cabernet Sauvignon, softer Merlots and Carmenères, Bordeaux blends, and smoky Pinotage.

MÉDOC

95   R

Mé

Médoc

A region within Bordeaux, France, situated on the left bank of the Gironde Estuary. Sometimes wines from here are called Médoc wines but more likely Bordeaux. The Médoc contains the most famous group of appellations, or defined wine regions, in the world in its Haut-Médoc (High Médoc) district. Though the wines from St-Estèphe, Pauillac, and St-Julien, as well as Margaux, garner much of the publicity, they represent a tiny proportion of Bordeaux wines. See also Bordeaux. Notably, the soil in this maritime region is gravelly, which suits Cabernet Sauvignon better than Merlot vines and is a key reason for the *châteaux* on this side of the Gironde to produce Cabernet Sauvignon–dominated dry red wines, though they are typically a blend of grapes, including Merlot, with perhaps some herbier Cabernet Franc or deeply colored Petit Verdot. Some of the wines were "officially classified" in 1855 as top growths, or *crus*, but the less well known usually offer better value. Look for red and black fruits, perhaps with some fresh herbs mingling with cigar-box aromas, and maybe a touch of smokiness and vanilla with medium alcohol levels in a medium to full body. Younger wines and Cabernet Sauvignon–strong Bordeaux can have chewier tannins, so serve with meats and cheeses and/or decant to soften and bring out the flavors, but the tannins will be softer and silky in older wines and where there is more Merlot in the blend. Look for the classic Bordeaux notes of woody herbs, graphite-pencil aromas, and minerality. Good to accompany main meals, roasts, casseroles, hard cheeses, and heartier vegetarian food. Also check out Cabernet Sauvignon and Merlots from elsewhere, Malbec, darker Cahors, Tannats with higher tannins, and smokier Pinotage.

Column 16

	96 R **Am** Amarone
88 G **Cs** Cabernet Sauvignon	**97** G **Cg** Carignan
89 G **Sy** Syrah	**98** G **Sh** Shiraz
90 R **Ce** Côte-Rôtie	**99** G **Zi** Zinfandel
91 G **Du** Durif	**100** G **Pr** Primitivo
92 R **Ba** Barolo	**101** G **Pv** Petit Verdot
93 G **Mv** Mourvèdre	**102** G **Ag** Aglianico
94 R **Ca** Cahors	**103** G **Ng** Negroamaro
95 R **Mé** Médoc	**104** G **Ta** Tannat

Many of these red wines are known to be bold, powerful, and hearty, with deep, brooding colors and flavors. They often benefit from longer aging, which softens their tannins, so look for older vintages and consider decanting before drinking. They can include dried fruits as well as ripe dark fruits, and these can be accompanied by spicy notes, often from the use of oak in the making and aging, but some of the grapes here are naturally spicy too. These wines are warming in the winter and make ideal partners for richer cuisine. Note: Sometimes winemakers use techniques that do not extract as much from the grapes to make a more approachable style of wine. This can be confusing, but brings in cash for the winemaker and enables him or her to use the best grapes in the bolder wines to age. If this style is made, it is normally less expensive and a good entry point.

AMARONE

Drying red Corvina grapes concentrates their flavors to make this full-bodied Venetian wine taste almost sweet. It is rich and ripe wine with a refreshing acidic tang. Amarones are bold encompassing flavors like chocolate, warm plums, morello cherries, dried fruits, coffee, and sweet spices, with a touch of rum and herbs. Alcohol is high—14 percent–plus ABV—to match the lingering big flavors, firm but velvety tannins, and complex layers. The best are aged in oak, giving complexity plus softness to the power, and they can keep at home. This indulgent style goes well with big cheeses and meaty dishes such as casseroles, and makes a warming winter drink. This is a wine to take your time over. (See Valpolicella for light, summer-sipping wines from the same region.) You might also like a slightly lighter *ripasso* style of Valpolicella, a fruity, ripe Zinfandel from the United States, Shiraz from

Australia, or the latter's GSM (Grenache, Syrah and Mourvèdre blend), Châteauneuf-du-Pape, and Ports.

CARIGNAN

A deeply colored red grape variety known as Cariñena in Spain, Carignane in the United States, and specifically as Mazuelo in Rioja. It has zippy acidity and hard, sometimes chewy, tannins, and is a touch rustic. Usually it is found blended with other grapes like Syrah, Grenache, and Mourvèdre, making a more harmonious style of wine. It adds red and blackberry flavors, as well as color, freshness, and tannin, and can impart dense, dark fruit—even figs—especially where grapes from old vines (*vieilles vignes*) are used; these wines are likely to be juicier and more concentrated. Look for names like the herby and rosemary-scented Corbières, Minervois, Faugères and other wines from the Languedoc. It is also used in Priorat, southern Italy, and in some wines from Chile. Its use is declining as there is a trend for more finesse in wine styles. Soften these wines by decanting or by keeping them for a while. A match for a range of strong flavors such as beef, lamb, aged game, and barbecues. Try also Durif, Syrah, and Shiraz, or for something smoother, a Malbec or Primitivo along with the riper Zinfandel.

SHIRAZ

A leading international deeply colored red grape variety, aka Syrah, where it is grown in cooler regions, which tend to be in the Old World, since the grape's characteristics and therefore style of the wine changes with climate. See also Syrah. New World Shiraz is riper, fruitier, and more full-bodied, with lower acidity, softer tannins, and a more viscous texture compared to Old World Syrah. It may have less pepper and more violet, chocolate, and coffee in hotter locations. Though less subtle and elegant, it is equally delicious. It has aromas and flavors of dark fruits like blackberries and plums and could have some black currants. This sunnier style of Shiraz is classically found in Australia, on its own and mixed with other varieties, perhaps showing a telltale note of eucalyptus. It has achieved worldwide success in California, South Africa (which makes both "styles" of the grape), Chile, and vineyards across Europe. Alcohol can be high, but it integrates and balances with the bold flavors, so check the label. A good match for herby or spicy lamb meals, meatballs, barbecue, and hard cheeses. You could also try Amarone, Zinfandel, Ripasso della Valpolicella, and wines from the southern Rhône.

ZINFANDEL

99	G
Zi	
Zinfandel	

An old, deep, and bold red grape variety, with a large acreage in California (see White Zinfandel, and also Primitivo). Zinfandel is intensely fruity and full of really ripe, dark cherries, sometimes even with dried fruit and chocolate flavors as well as high alcohol—sometimes very high, so read the label. Wines are full-bodied, with an unctuous texture, especially where they have been aged in oak, which softens and further rounds out the wine as well as adding vanilla and spicy tones, and is intense where the vines are old (*vieilles*). High alcohol and tannin levels tend to be hidden by the power of the wine. Primitivos from Puglia in the heel of Italy are thought to be the same grape, with more herby, earthy tones plus higher acidity. Surprisingly, this is a good match for Thanksgiving dinner, harmonizing with all the trimmings, also big barbecue and big cheeses. If you like these rich, juicy Zins, try also Italian Primitivo, Amarone, the slightly lighter Ripasso della Valpolicella, or a spicy Shiraz.

PRIMITIVO

A southern Italian red wine grape with spicy black currant and raspberry flavors and at times wild berries, mingling with violets and dried figs. It opens out when left in the glass. It can be medium but tends to be full-bodied, with a round, plush texture. Some are more rustic than others, depending on the fineness of the high level of tannins and the age of the vines used. It is known as Zinfandel in California. Acidity is higher than the more unctuous California Zinfandel, which can make it easier-drinking and helps with flexibility in food pairing. Fuller styles are sunny with ripe, dark, cherry, and sometimes chocolate flavors. Alcohol can be high, so check the label. This style of wine needs food, so try a plate of pasta, especially Bolognese, generously dusted with savory Parmesan and black pepper, or match with barbecued ribs. One to taste if you haven't already. See Zinfandel. Other wines to try are Italian Aglianico and Negroamaro, plus Châteauneuf-du-Pape, Shiraz, and Durif.

PETIT VERDOT

A deeply colored, tannic red grape variety that is used predominantly as a minority element of the blend in Bordeaux wines, especially for wines made on the left bank of the Gironde Estuary. It may not even appear on the label as it is added as "a dash of," like seasoning, rather than as a large dollop. Even so, in this capacity it has the strength to bring color and tannin as well as spice (pencil shavings and sometimes molasses), floral perfume notes, acidity, and alcohol. However, it does not always ripen fully, and when this occurs it can be a touch green (nettles rather than herbs). Due to its Bordeaux connection, Petit Verdot is found around the globe, where it is less likely to struggle to ripen and still plays a role in Cabernet Sauvignon and Merlot blends. In the New World, riper grapes are more likely to be flying solo, but the wines are still tricky to find; these more generous wines will be deeper-colored, richer, and fuller-bodied with darker fruit flavors like black plums accompanied by scents of violets. When mixed with oak, which softens the high tannins, tar, coffee, and leather notes emerge. If there is enough information on a label, try Bordeaux blends with differing amounts of Petit Verdot; occasionally it is mixed with the Rhône grape Syrah too.

AGLIANICO

Serious, full-bodied, alcoholic, sun-loving, southern Italian, heavy, and deeply colored red grape. The best grows in volcanic soil, which adds freshness as well as a flash of chalky minerality to its weight. Found in Taurasi in the Campania region and Aglianico del Vulture in neighboring Basilicata, Aglianico wines are all damson plum and black currant, with a mineral edge. In youth it has more crunchy fruits, with wisps of violet perfume and vivid purple colors. Usually made with oak, but rosso-labeled and unoaked wines can be a lighter and more affordable introduction to the grape variety. Aglianico can be tannic, so let it breathe or decant to soften before tasting. However, along with power, Aglianico wines can offer finesse, and some age well. Older wines, usually made using oak, enjoy finer, not-so-drying tannins as well as a more viscous, generous texture; there are also layers of ashy smokiness, licorice with vanilla, blackberries, and a lingering finish. Vintage, or year of production, can be important. The acidity, flavors, and usually high alcohol make this a wine to drink with food like hearty beef dishes, barbecues and warming autumnal and winter fare. Try also big Italian Primitivo or Zinfandel in California.

NEGROAMARO

Negroamaro is a red wine grape and important local variety grown in the Puglia region in the heel of Italy. It is deeply colored, with medium to high tannins and body, depending on how it is made. It can be a varietal wine but is also found blended with Primitivo and Malvasia grapes. Occasionally it is gently pressed to make a lighter-styled (compared to the red wines), summer-fruited, cherry-colored dry rosé which includes flavors of red berries, pomegranates, and cherries and can have a mineral note of flint, depending on the vineyard soil, or a yogurt note from lees (dead yeast cells) stirring. Rosés are produced for drinking when young and fruity. Reds are available in a spectrum of styles, from more rustic but approachable, to finer and more serious, reflected in the prices. The Mediterranean sunshine provides vibrant, rich, nutmeg-spiced wines, sometimes with strawberry coulis but more likely robust body with plums, soft blackberries when young, and more intense currants and chocolate flavors, plus attractive aromas of licorice, cloves, and rich coffee. Alcohol levels can be high. Look for names like Salice Salentino and others such as Brindisi and Copertino. With good levels of acidity, Negroamaro is delicious served with dishes like meatballs, lamb, and grilled tuna. The rosés complement Mediterranean meals garnished with black olives. Also try Cabernet Sauvignon, the more tannic Aglianico, Tannat, and Cahors.

TANNAT

A red wine grape that makes deeply colored, inky, dry, and rustic wine with high alcohol levels and mineral aromas of tar along with black fruit flavors such as damson, plum, and blackberries. "Black wines" from Madiran in southwest France are made with a majority of Tannat blended with the Cabernets (Franc and Sauvignon), so have a touch of leafiness about them.

It is also successful in Uruguay, where wines can be a touch lower in tannins, but this is all relative. High in natural acidity, with chewy tannins, Tannat is blended too, but with the likes of less rustic Merlot and Cabernet Sauvignon and even Pinot Noir. Softening winemaking techniques are often employed, or maybe just aging the wine. These methods, as well as a sensitive use of oak, are bringing about a change to modernize Tannat so that it produces a more harmonious and balanced wine. Decanting can help this process at home. Aged wines cost more and continue the black theme, with aromas of prunes, chocolate, and cloves. Pair this wine with sociable rustic fare that boasts dark, concentrated flavors like lamb with a reduced balsamic vinegar sauce, beefy bangers and mash, or mature cheddar and caramelized onion sandwiches. Other dark wines to try are Aglianico, Negroamaro, Cahors, Carignan, and Durif. Cabernet Sauvignon is fruitier, less tannic, and more approachable. Nebbiolo wines, like Barolo, have the tar, with a scattering of roses but a pale color.

Sparkling

All these sparkling wines have bubbles and are made in regions renowned for the excellence of their fizz. There is diversity within this category, from pale and sweet to deep and lingering. Note how the manner in which the bubbles are created in the wine changes in different regions; simply pumping carbon dioxide into a still wine has no place in any of these quality appellations.

ASTI

Asti is a hilly province in Piedmont, northwest Italy. It gives its name to gentle, sweet, often fun and frivolous pale sparkling wines that used to be known as Asti Spumante. Asti (as it is now known) is made using the floral, orange-blossom, and grapy Muscat grape, whose qualities winemakers wish to preserve and highlight. The special Asti production method encapsulates this fruity, flowery, candylike perfumed freshness while simultaneously adding bubbles and retaining some of the grapes' natural sugars. (The bubbles in some sparkling wines are added to a previously made still wine.) The youthful wine is therefore low in alcohol and sweet, but should be fresh and vibrant, as the hillside location of the vineyards helps keep acidity in the grapes as well as harnessing the sunshine. Astis are slightly less fizzy than Champagne. Drink these lacy wines immediately, otherwise their vivacity and aromas fade and they become sickly. This is not a wine to keep. Serve chilled with meringues, fruit salads, and other fruit-based desserts. Wines labeled "Moscato d'Asti" are lighter: lower alcohol and sweeter. See also Moscato. In other places in the world, similar Moscato-styled sparkling wine are available, usually with slightly riper flavors; some are rose-colored too. These include a layer of red fruits—lovely with strawberry and raspberry desserts. Try also drier, higher-alcohol Prosecco, and if you would like a Champagne or similar from outside that region, choose a wine labeled *"demi-sec,"* as this will have some sweetness as well as some biscuity layers that result from the different production method.

106 G
Mo
Moscato

MOSCATO

Moscato is the Italian name for the perfumed Muscat grape. On the label of a sparkling wine from Piedmont, Italy, it usually refers to Moscato d'Asti (see Asti); however, this entry recognizes that there are also similarly styled sparkling wine (called simply "Moscato" on the label) made across the globe, including other places in Italy outside the Asti region, as well as further afield in, for example, Australia, California, and South Africa. They are often light-bodied, easy-sipping, sweet but not overly so wines that are usually pale, almost white, and sometimes cotton-candy-colored. These acacia-honeyed wines mix floral orange-blossom and peachy flavors. Rosés involve cherry, strawberry and raspberry layers too.

Confusingly they can be found in a range of sweetness and fizziness levels. The more usual are only lightly sparkling with low-alcohol styles that are ideal as a refreshing summer sipper, well chilled alongside fruit-based desserts. Weightier wines can complement aromatic, spicy Asian food and light cheeses. The shape of the bottle can hint at the style of the wine: i.e., its levels of sweetness, alcohol, and fizziness. Those in Champagne-shaped bottles are fizzy, while those in a "normal," straight-sided, Bordeaux-shaped bottle tend to be less fizzy. If you see lower alcohol on the label, this often means a touch more sweetness. Note that because Muscat is an adaptable grape, some sparkling Moscatos are dry; look for *"secco"* on the label and higher alcohol levels. See also Muscat, which covers the still styles of wine made from the versatile and prolific grape variety. Try also Proseccos, which are drier sparkling wines but not as floral nor honeyed and perhaps a little zingier. For a swap to a still wine you might also like white Zinfandel, or, for more finesse, a *Kabinett*. Try Riesling from Germany for a similar, low-alcohol, off-dry still wine.

PROSECCO

The name of a popular, joyous, lemon-sherbet-tinged sparkling white wine created in Italy near Venice from Glera grapes. Proseccos are produced using a method known as charmat that retains all the fresh fruit, green apple, and melon qualities of the grapes—which is partly why Proseccos are fruitier than Champagnes (the different grape varieties used in both wines also play a big part). Here bubbles are formed in a still wine by a second fermentation in a large tank. The light, refreshing sparkling wine is bottled ready for immediate consumption. The charmat method is also suitable for other aromatic grapes. Proseccos labeled *"frizzante"* are less fizzy than the customary fully sparkling *spumante* wines; *"spumante"* does not always appear on the label. Alcohol is usually a touch lower than in Champagne and sweetness levels vary. Unless it specifically states otherwise on the label, any sugar is counterbalanced by the wine's freshness, so Proseccos are not cloying but have a light, refreshing quality. If the label mentions "DOCG," rather than "DOC," it indicates a higher quality classification, and the wine will have more layers of flavor, linger longer, and contain finer bubbles, which create a silky sensation in the mouth. Expect to pay a little more for DOCG, although generally this is still a more affordable bubbly than Champagne. If you are planning on making a peachy Bellini cocktail, or adding orange juice for a breakfast treat, plain old DOC Prosecco is all that is required. Similarly styled wines are made around the globe, though they cannot use the Prosecco name on the label. Drink them chilled, young, and fresh as an aperitif or for an impromptu midweek celebration.

CAVA

Cava is the name of a sparkling wine made using the same traditional method as Champagne but in Spain and usually with different grape varieties. Most is made in the northeast, near Barcelona, although Cava can come from many areas in the country. Cava is typically a non-vintage wine containing a blend of indigenous Spanish grapes, while a few producers draw on grapes like Chardonnay and Pinot Noir that are used in Champagne. *Rosado* (rosé) coloring comes from the skins of Garnacha (Grenache) and Monastrell grapes. Like Champagne, the bubbles in Cava are created naturally during a second fermentation in the bottle, and the wine spends a significant amount of time maturing in the bottle. In this way, layers of biscuit, dough, and a touch of cream-like flavors are added to the fruit flavors. Cava typically has a mineral aroma reminiscent of smoke or a rubber balloon. Serve these dry, refreshing, medium-alcohol, more modestly priced sparkling wines chilled as an aperitif, with smoked salmon canapés, seafood, some Catalonian cuisine and in cocktails. Naturally, also try Champagne and other sparkling wines from around the world made using the *metodo tradicional*, but for something fruitier without the creamy notes, turn to Prosecco.

CRÉMANT

French sparkling wine, from regions other than Champagne, made using the same *méthode champenoise* (aka *méthode traditionelle* outside the Champagne region), *crémants* are usually non-vintage and made with local grapes, which may or may not be the Champagne grapes Chardonnay, Pinot Noir, and Pinot Meunier. Typically, the region of production appears in the name: Crémant d'Alsace, Crémant de Bourgogne, Crémant de Limoux, and so on. Saumur *mousseux* and sparkling Vouvrays are normally better quality than the Crémant de Loire from the same region. Generally produced to be enjoyed young, fruity, and fresh, these sparkling wines are still zippy but with less of the bread, biscuit, and dough layers usually found in Champagne. If made using a local grape, a hint of its flavor profile comes through. They are often crafted by famous Champagne houses which bring their skills and backing to the *crémant*, which means these wines can be a good-value alternative to Champagne. Most are, like Champagne, white wines; however, rosés with more red fruits (rarely red) are made. Alcohol is medium. Other countries make sparkling wine using the *méthode traditionelle*; in Germany these are called Deutscher Sekt; in South Africa, Cap Classique; in Italy, Franciacorta. In the New World, California, Australia, and New Zealand, look for "Traditional Method" on the label and expect slightly riper fruit flavors.

CHAMPAGNE

A cool region toward the north of France after which its celebratory sparkling wines are named. Three permitted grapes—Chardonnay, Pinot Noir, and Pinot Meunier—are used. The latter two are red, but the delicate pressing of the grapes is so gentle that color is not extracted from their skins, making the vast majority of Champagnes white, with only a few rosés. The *méthode champenoise* dictates that bubbles must be made inside the bottle. Yeast and sugar are added to the bottled still wine, which starts a second fermentation. Here the carbon dioxide is created but is trapped in the sealed bottle, and *voilà*! There is fizz. In the best this is smooth, silky, and fine and far removed from the big, short-lived, bursting bubbles of carbonated soda. This process takes time, however, so this in part accounts for the premium prices of this special drink. Different Champagne houses—the brands—have their own styles: some young and quite zippy and sharp, others aged, softer, and creamier. Find a style you prefer. Alcohol is at the medium level. Sweetness levels range from bone-dry to lusciously sweet *doux* styles. Usually Champagnes are dry to just off-dry *bruts*, which match savory canapés well. To pair with a dessert or cake choose sweet *demi-sec* wines. There are few other label terms to understand to get the most out of this drink, which is more often than not consumed to mark a special occasion. "Non-vintage" means the wine is a blend of years, which helps ensure a consistent "house style"; they are usually released ready to drink, not aged. Vintage Champagnes are made with grapes from a single particularly good harvest. They spend longer aging—often much more than the minimum. This style of Champagne is richer, more honeyed, and lingering and can include both savory and fruity tones. *Blanc de blancs* Champagne is made solely from white grapes, giving more citrus and green apple hints, becoming buttery if aged. *Blanc de noirs* sparkling wine is made from red grapes only; you may detect a hint of richer red fruits.

LAMBRUSCO

A red wine grape that gives its name to fizzy Italian wines made mostly in the Emilia-Romagna region. The name became synonymous with mass-produced, low-alcohol, simple, sickly, dark-pink sparkling wine. It is worth noting that, although hard to find, the best Lambruscos must be made using a second fermentation to make the bubbles in the bottle—like the method used to make Champagne—so be sure to check the label. A little easier to discover are quality Lambruscos that are created in a similar way to Prosecco. Alcohol and fizz may be a touch lower than in other sparkling wines. These deep-crimson, quality wines are dry, succulent, and bursting with red cherries, a hint of violets, and refreshing acidity plus herby tannins and a touch of tobacco. Tannins and a touch of bitterness on the finish make them food-friendly. Rosé and white versions are less common, and contain little or no tannins. Delicious when slightly cooled—even the reds— as an accompaniment to flavorsome charcuterie like Parma ham, salami, and other rich, savory delicatessen delights; also a good foil for roast turkey: think vinous cranberry sauce. Be surprised and try one of these.

SPARKLING SHIRAZ

112   S
Ss
**Sparkling
Shiraz**

Sparkling Shiraz is a deeply colored sparkling Australian red wine made from juicy Shiraz (Syrah) grapes. The best winemakers rein in the potential for it to be big, brash, overbubbly, oaky, and alcoholic, assimilating its best characteristics into a full-bodied and harmonious balance. With a touch of the rebel about them, these wines are weighty and rich, tasting of red berries, blackberries, a touch of violets, and peppery spice, with smoke on the finish. Sparkling Shiraz offers red currant–like fresh acidity combined with smooth tannins and moussey bubbles. Alcohol can be medium to high. A little bit of oak can soften the wine and if aged, chocolate, meaty, leathery, and savory notes develop, although the price increases. Good with barbecue, roast turkey and cranberry sauce, duck, and some game. Those that are off-dry can even pair with a rich chocolate cake.

Sweet

All these sweeties have something in common: a concentration and intensity of flavors that offset the natural sweetness of the grape juice itself. No sugar is added. Drink with equally sweet food to create balance and harmony. High-acidity wines can cut through rich desserts and are refreshing, not cloying, to drink. Dry wines can taste thin or bitter alongside sweet cuisine.

113	R
Iw	
Icewine	

ICEWINE

A type of dessert wine most famously made in Canada and Germany, where it is known as Eiswein, although other countries make it too. Icewine is made from grapes that are left hanging on the vines for a very long time, well into the winter (usually grapes are harvested in early autumn). Grapes destined for Icewine are left until it is so cold that the water inside them freezes, then they are hand-picked, often at night. Pressing these frozen dry grapes (raisins) removes concentrated sugary grape juice that is so rich that after fermentation the wine remains naturally and intensely sweet. The frozen water and ice crystals are not used. These time-consuming practices and the low yields mean Icewine has a premium price tag, and tends to be fuller-bodied compared to wines where grapes are harvested in late autumn. The clean flavors depend on the grape variety used. Typically, Riesling is used in Germany, while in Canada both white grapes, such as Vidal and Riesling, and red grapes, such as Cabernet Franc, are used. Expect especially pure, sharp flavors of tropical fruits, peaches, honey, citrus, melon, and strawberries, with a balanced backbone of acidity. Serve chilled with an ice bucket. Icewine pairs well with chocolate or fruit desserts, and strongly flavored savories like pâté and blue cheeses. Try also sweet Riesling from Austria, Tokaji from Hungary, and more affordable late-harvest dessert wines from around the world.

VIN SANTO

A concentrated, Italian sweet "holy wine" made all over the country and famously associated with Tuscany. The intensity of Vin Santo results partly from drying the grapes, traditionally on straw mats in the sun or winery, for up to six months before gently fermenting the raisined fruit. These variable sweet wines are mainly a blend of white Malvasia and Trebbiano grapes, sometimes with Sangiovese or other varieties. Pale straw to rich amber in color, these wines are put in small barrels to age untouched in lofts for at least three years. Evaporation through the wood, plus the gentle movement of oxygen into these barrels, adds to the intensity as well as layers of flavors and aromas or complexity. Think scents and flavors of apricots, raisins, dried figs, and acacia honey. These can evolve into toasted nuts and caramel or toffee given age, as unopened wines can keep. Vin Santo wines are a touch viscous in texture, with crisp acidity, so the sweetness is not cloying; however, sweetness levels do vary depending on the winemaker; dolce is the sweetest. Alcohol is around 16 percent ABV. Occasionally fortified—look for "*liquoroso*" on the label—with a touch higher alcohol. Serve cool, classically with biscotti, and with desserts like cheesecake and buttery pastries. You could also try Vin Santo from Greece, Madeira, white Port, or Muscat de Beaumes-de-Venise for something more floral and less nutty, Sauternes for more marmalade notes, and aged *demi-sec* Champagne for bubbles and lighter alcohol.

TOKAJI

Tokaj is a region in northern Hungary that gives its name, as Tokaji, to golden, refreshing, medium-bodied white dessert wines made predominantly from botrytised (affected by botrytis, a mold otherwise known as "noble rot"; see Sauternes for more information) Furmint grapes. The winemaking method is similar to that of Sauternes, with the additional process of steeping nobly rotten, or *aszú*, grapes in a still wine. This infusion brings layers of both freshness and maturity, integrating them in a single wine. Look for "*puttonyos*" on the label; this indicates the grade of sweetness, so the higher the *puttonyos* number, the sweeter the style. All types of Tokaji should have balanced, refreshing, citrus acidity; four *puttonyos* is the most commonly available. A gentle use of oak adds vanilla and creamy hints to the apricot, spicy citrus, and white-blossom flavors as well as a silky texture. Enjoy chilled with cakes, peaches, pâté, and smoked fish, and as a treat during celebratory meals. Also sip Sauternes, dessert Rieslings from Germany and Austria, apple-y Vouvrays, and more aromatic Sauvignon Blanc dessert wines from Chile and Australia.

SAUTERNES

116	R
Sa	
Sauternes	

A village in Bordeaux, southwest France, that gives its name to honey-colored, medium-bodied white dessert wines from that region and appellation. Made predominantly from white Sémillon grapes that have been left to hang on the vines to develop more layers of flavor and become affected by the intensifying noble rot (botrytis). A touch of Sauvignon Blanc gives the wine a lift and brightness, and alcohol tends to be around 14 percent ABV. Noble rot is a type of friendly mold that compromises the skin of the grapes, allowing evaporation. The remaining grape juice inside the berries becomes more concentrated, complex, and luscious. This adds marmalade notes to flavors of acacia honey and tropical fruits, and these combine with zesty citrus flavors and a good level of refreshing acidity, which balances the sweetness so that the wine is not cloying. More affordable wines are bottled for drinking soon after release and in half-size bottles. The pricier bottles can age; they deepen in color, eventually turning almost amber with time and adding darker honey, dried fruit, and savory aromas and flavors. Enjoy chilled with crème brûlée, tarte au citron, rich egg custards, tarte tatin, and blue cheeses. From the same region though more affordable, try Barsac, Ste-Croix-du-Mont, and further afield, Montbazillac, Tokaji from Hungary and dessert Sauvignon Blancs from Chile and Australia. More straightforward, floral, and youthful, sip Muscat de St-Jean de Minervois. For a more apple-y style, try sweet Vouvrays and dessert Rieslings from Germany and Austria.

BANYULS

A commune on the Mediterranean coast in the southeast of Roussillon called Banyuls-sur-Mer gives its name to full-bodied fortified red wines. Similar to ruby and late-bottled vintage ports, Banyuls is made from local Grenache grapes that thrive in this hot, windy region of southern France on the border with Spain. In France, this style is called *vin doux naturel* (or VDN: "naturally sweet wine"), referring to the adding of grape spirit during fermentation. This stops the yeast from fermenting any more of the sugar from the red grapes, resulting in a full-bodied, fruity wine with reasonable tannin levels. Alcohol levels tend to be lower than in ports—about 16 percent ABV.

Like Port, there is a range of styles from the younger and fruitier to the aged versions, which are more complex and show dried fruits and nuts—more like a tawny Port style. VDNs can also be a touch more herbal, with light floral notes, when a seasoning of Muscat grapes is used. Delicious on its own or paired with chocolate-based desserts and red fruit compotes of morello cherries and poached strawberries, blackberries, and raspberries. You might also like Maury, made close by, and Rasteau, plus the lighter, more amber-colored Rivesaltes—all from France. Commandaria from Cyprus, Mavrodaphne from Greece, and some fortified wines from Australia are similar in style too. For a dry red wine with similar full body and alcohol, try neighboring Collioure and Châteauneuf-du-Pape.

MAURY

A commune in Roussillon that gives its name to full-bodied, fortified wines that are usually red, although rosé and whites are made too. Similar to ruby and late-bottled vintage ports, Maury dessert wines are made from Grenache grapes that thrive in this hot, windy region of southern France. In France, this style is called *vin doux naturel* (VDN: "naturally sweet wine"), and is made by adding grape spirit during fermentation, leaving a full-bodied, fruity wine with reasonable tannin levels. Alcohol levels tend to be around 15–17 percent ABV—lower than for ports.

Like Port, there is a range of styles, from younger, tannic, fruitier, plummy wines to aged, complex, savory examples full of dried fruits and roasted nuts plus a dash of cedar, coffee, and chocolate. Maury VDNs are riper and more herbal than Port and are good on their own, but also lovely paired with figs and blue cheese, mince pies, and dark, moist fruit or walnut cakes, or with a coffee and chocolate at the end of a meal. If you like this style, you could also try Banyuls, made close by, and Rasteau, also from France; Commandaria from Cyprus and Mavrodaphne from Greece, and some fortified wines from Australia are similar in style too. For a dry red wine with similar full body and alcohol, try the sec version of Maury, Châteauneuf-du-Pape, and its neighboring appellations like Lirac. If you prefer nuts and licorice flavors, try Pedro Ximénez Sherry.

Fortified

These wines come in a variety of colors ranging from pale lemon to almost black, with sweetness levels ranging from bone-dry to sweet, and they offer a myriad of flavors, from lasting, fresh and fruity to lingering, deep, dark and viscous. Extra alcohol added during the production process changes the characteristics as well as increasing the alcohol in the final wine.

Sherry can only come from Jerez in southern Spain, and is made using mainly white Palomino grapes. Port can only come from the Douro Valley region of Portugal and is made using a blend of highly colored red grapes local to the region. Similarly, Madeira can only come from the island after which it is named. A variety of styles is available in all these fortified wines because of the long history of winemaking in these regions. To help highlight and clarify the diversity of these wines, Sherry and Port in particular occupy more than one cell. Find out more for yourself by trying the diverse styles of fortified wines.

FINO SHERRY

119   R

Fs

Fino Sherry

Fino sherries are the pale-colored, bone-dry, generally tangy, and lip-smacking varieties, bursting with citrus notes like lemon juice and zest, pithy grapefruit, and fresh, nutty almonds. Finos are made using a *solera*, a maturation system that creates complex blends of wines from different years. A special native Spanish yeast called *flor* helps imbue these zippy aperitifs with yeasty dough notes too. Typically alcohol is around 15 percent ABV. These light wines are fresh, designed to be consumed chilled soon after release, plus within a few days of opening; otherwise, they become tired-tasting and dull. Winemakers also produce other styles of fino-based sherries. Fino sherries are sometimes salty, a good example being Manzanillas, which are finos that are produced closer to the Spanish coast. Manzanillas are the palest of the finos, and very tangy and saline in flavor because of their proximity to the sea. "Pale cream" sherries are fino sherries that have been sweetened using concentrated grape juice. All of these lighter-styled sherries make a perfect accompaniment for salted almonds and tapas dishes and can stand up to really savory, flavorsome meals with plenty of umami notes like fish and chips, as the tanginess of the wine makes taste buds water.

OLOROSO SHERRY

A deep, amber-colored, walnutty, dry, dark style of Sherry, olorosos are produced from the same white Palomino grapes that are used to make light styles such as fino. They start life as light still wines, which are fortified to around 17 percent ABV—a higher strength than for a fino Sherry. This kills the special protective blanket of Spanish Sherry yeast (*flor*). The wine is then left to mature in partially full old barrels. This means oxygen works with the wine, gradually deepening the color and creating flavors such as leather, toffee, spices, and nuts; the wine becomes richer, quite full-bodied, and weightier in the mouth. The longer the aging, the more intense dried-fruit flavors that develop (think dates and figs), and alcohol levels increase to around 20 percent ABV or more. Winemakers also produce other styles of darker sherries. Amontillado sherries are a halfway mix between fino and oloroso. They have a touch more alcohol than finos and in flavor profile are halfway between pale fino and nutty oloroso with an amber hue. If sweetened, they are called "medium Sherry." Cream sherries are typically oloroso sherries sweetened with concentrated grape juice. These sweeter styles accompany fruit and walnut cakes, plus caramel and nut-based desserts such as pecan pie. Dry olorosos pair well with more meaty and savory tapas and even pork stews and sausages and mashed potatoes with rich onion gravy.

MADEIRA

This Portuguese island in the Atlantic Ocean gives its name to fortified wines that range in sweetness levels from dry, refreshing, and nutty aperitifs to sweet, dried-fruit types that pair well with desserts such as fruitcake and pudding—and all styles in between. Note that not all Madeiras are sweet. These often fragrant and nutty wines start life as a still wine that has Portuguese grape spirit added to it to bring the alcohol level to around 20 percent ABV. Next, and unusually, the wine is exposed to gentle heat for a long period (this would ruin most wine). Because the wines are stored in barrels, air enters, which oxidizes the contents. Colors darken and flavors intensify to dried fruit, nuts, orange zest, and coffee notes. This heating means a Madeira wine will keep for a reasonably long time without spoiling once opened (unlike most wines, which need to be consumed soon after opening)—handy for an occasional sip. Madeira styles vary from the sweeter, richer Malmsey and slightly less rich Bual to the drier Sercial and off-dry Verdelho. These are also the names of the white grapes used to make each style of Madeira, so look for them on Madeira wine labels. The range of styles and their mouth-watering acidity means Madeiras pair well with a variety of dishes. Added to gravy, they make a roast dinner taste extra-special. These wines work well with mushroom-based sauces, with sweeter styles complementing dark chocolate puddings, brownies, nutty flans, and ice cream.

RUTHERGLEN MUSCAT

Rutherglen is a hot region in Victoria, Australia, after which this sweet, amber-hued, fortified dessert wine is named. Muscat grapes are partially dried, or raisined, by leaving them hanging on the vines in the heat. Their pure, concentrated juice starts fermenting. Spirit is added during the fermentation process, which halts it, so natural sweetness remains. These "stickies," as they are known, taste of raisins and ripe grapes, with floral flavors like rose petal, as well as fruit cake, citrus zest, and sweet baking spice notes combined with a luscious, viscous texture. Alcohol is around 17 percent ABV. The youngest wines are most readily available and simplest in flavor. Other longer-aged styles are made by maturing in wood, usually under hot tin roofs, and also using a *solera* system (which blends wines of different ages, like in Sherry production). These are more intense and nuttier, with treacle tones and higher levels of alcohol. Serve chilled with mince pies, dark fruit cakes, and matured cheeses. Try other sweet wines like Madeira, Tokaji, or Vin Santo, and maybe a tawny Port.

PEDRO XIMÉNEZ

123   G
Px
Pedro
Ximénez

The name of a white grape grown across Spain and used in Andalucia as "the second" Sherry grape. It is used both to name and make this dark, rich, viscous, sweet Sherry, which is a complete contrast to other styles— hence it gets its own listing here. Pedro Ximénez, or PX, Sherry is made from sun-dried bunches of grapes left until they raisin. The concentrated remaining juice is partially fermented, then neutral high-alcohol spirit is added, which stops the process. The wine is matured in the *solera* system of barrels, which allows complex blending across years to create a consistent quality product with layers of flavors. Alcohol level is about 16 percent ABV. The result is an unctuously sweet, dark-brown wine, bursting with flavors of figs, dried fruits, molasses, citrus zest, marmalade, licorice, and prunes that evolve in the mouth as it is sipped. Deliciously intense when savored on its own, drop by drop, or, classically, poured over vanilla ice cream.

RUBY PORT

A full-bodied, fruity, youthful, fortified, deep-red wine made in the Douro region of Portugal from a blend of robust, deeply colored local grapes. It is aged for a relatively short time: two to three years in large oak vats. Rubies are straightforward, sweet, rich red wines with flavors of concentrated, ripe, crunchy red plums and other berries, sometimes with a hint of flowers. Alcohol is around 20 percent ABV and can be more fiery than in tawny Port. Similarly tannins tend to be more noticeable. Reserve ports are comparable but are higher quality as they are aged for slightly longer. Fine rubies are more affordable and less complex. This Port style is released to be consumed rather than age further, and does not need to be decanted before drinking as the Port is filtered before bottling. See also Late-Bottled Vintage Ports. Good with nuts and chocolate puddings, plus the sweetness enhances salty food, including the classic Stilton cheese.

LATE-BOTTLED VINTAGE PORT

A full-bodied, tannic, and complex sweet, fortified, deep-red wine made in Portugal. The deeply colored red grapes are indigenous to the Douro River region. Late-bottled vintage (LBV) ports use a blend of grapes from a single declared vintage (year) only. This occurs only once every few years. Similar to the more prestigious vintage Port, LBVs spend much more time in large casks before being bottled; this makes them approachable to drink earlier, as the tannins soften and flavors integrate during this time. They are more affordable too. The sweetness comes from the grapes, which do not totally ferment due to the addition, or "fortification," of the wine with high-strength neutral grape spirit. LBVs are richer, well-rounded, and with more layers of flavor compared to ruby ports; they are also fruitier but less complex than vintage ports and without the nutty and savory hints of a tawny Port. Alcohol, like other ports, is around 20 percent ABV. "Traditional" on the label means it will need decanting before drinking; otherwise LBVs are ready to drink. Tannins can be high, but drink with hard cheeses or meat platters to round them out in the mouth, plus try with hot chocolate puddings. Sample also Banyuls and Maury.

TAWNY PORT

A rich, mellow style of medium to full-bodied sweet, fortified red wine that has been aged in large casks in the Douro region of Portugal, before being bottled ready to drink. Named after its classic reddish-tawny hue that fades further in older wines. The cask-aging allows oxygen to permeate the wine: hence the faded color and more nutty, dried-fruit, "oxidative" flavors and aroma profile. Unlike vintage ports, tawnies do not need to be decanted, nor will they improve with keeping. They can be served cool—i.e., at "cellar temperature"—with more flavors evolving as they warm in the mouth. Sweetness and alcohol are balanced by a soft, red fruitiness, nuts and fruit-cake spices, and lingering flavors. Older tawnies are more about nuts, dried fruits, butterscotch, and softer tannins but come with higher prices. Younger ones show fresher red fruits and are more affordable. A ten-year-old tawny is a mix of the two flavor profiles that please most. Alcohol is usually around 20 percent ABV. A good match for hard, nutty cheeses like manchego, salty nuts, and desserts made with chocolate, figs, baked oranges, and crème brûlée, though the rarer, more expensive old categories are best savored, sip by sip, on their own.

127   R

Vp

Vintage Port

VINTAGE PORT

A full-bodied, tannic, and complex fortified, deeply colored, sweet, big red wine made in Portugal. Like all ports, the red grapes are indigenous to the Douro River region. For these vintage ports, grapes come from a single vintage (year) that is of an "officially declared" high quality. This only occurs once every few years; for some years no vintage Port is made at all. The superior grapes are rapidly turned into a deeply colored still red wine, but, before the fermentation is complete, a neutral brandy spirit is added to "fortify" the wine. This halts the fermentation, resulting in a high-alcohol red wine that is naturally sweet, as some of the sugar from the grapes remains in the wine.

Vintage is the most concentrated of all ports. It spends only a couple of years in large casks before being bottled and left to mature, integrating and softening as it does so. It is this full-bodied style of Port that should age for years, even decades, before layers of red and dried fruits, chocolate, and zesty, sweet spice all meld together and the tannins become velvety. The Port is only then ready to drink, and not until after decanting into another vessel without transferring the sediment that has built up during the maturation process. This decanting softens the wine further. Alcohol, like other ports, is around 20 percent ABV. Tannins can be high, especially when drunk too young. Traditionally drunk after dinner, this special-occasion beverage should not be rushed so as to appreciate its many layers, texture, and length of flavor.

Further reading

Sources of sipping information are readily accessible. There is plenty on the Internet, as well as apps to help you find out about individual wines, plus sections in most newspapers and magazines, often with topical recommendations or good offers to try. The more you combine tasting with reference, the deeper your interest and knowledge will become. Many of the references mentioned have helped with this book; some are included as further signposts for additional places to look.

Books   These are brilliant for beginners as they recommend specific bottles of wine to try from particular areas of the world:

500 White Wines by Natasha Hughes and Patricia Langton
500 Red Wines by Christine Austin
Wine & Spirit Education Trust books, from beginners to advanced levels. Plus, the Trust runs all sorts of courses, from tastings for beginners to serious wine enthusiasts.
Wine Grapes by Jancis Robinson, Julia Harding, and José Vouillamoz. This is a superb book, geeky and bursting with detail about 1,368 individual wine varieties, their history, and characteristics. More grapes than you'll ever need to know about! One for the real enthusiasts.

Websites   Many retailers, like liquor stores and wine shops, have really informative websites. Some include large amounts of free helpful information over and above a snappy description of the wine. A number offer courses or tastings, and if you are passing, they all have helpful staff who will be only too glad to talk to you about wine.

wine-searcher.com—Provides the latest wine news and prices plus information about regions and grape varieties.

winefolly.com—A good way to learn about wine supported by fabulous clear pictures.

decanter.com—Dedicated to wine, includes a magazine, fairs, tastings and trips.

thewinesociety.com—You can join the Wine Society to have access to good wine at good prices; viewing the informative website is free.

jancisrobinson.com—Offers a wealth of information about wine, grapes, regions and tasting notes. Some is free; paying to join gives you access to a long history of articles and comment. Robinson has collaborated with Hugh Johnson to write *The World Atlas of Wine*, which can be viewed via the site too.

Many wine regions have their own websites to guide you through the grapes, history and characteristics of the area:

bordeaux.com
bourgogne-wines.com
vinsvaldeloire.fr
vinhoverde.pt/en/vinhoverde
winesfromspainuk.com
winesofportugal.info
discovercaliforniawines.co.uk
languedoc-wines.com
rhone-wines.com
wineaustralia.com
austrianwine.com

Look for logos indicating that a wine has been judged an International Wine & Spirit Competition (IWSC) and/ or an International Wine Challenge (IWC) medal-winner.

Index

Acknowledgments

I would like to thank the following people who have inspired me along the way: The Wine & Spirit Education Trust (WSET), Michelle Cherutti-Kowal, Anne McHale, Nina Cerullo, Godfrey Spence, Christopher Donaldson, Andrew Jefford, Michael Walpole, and Emma Symington. With special thanks to Rosie Reynolds and Laura Higginson, plus the team at Ebury, without whom this project would not have come to fruition.

A toast to you all.

About the Author

After leaving her job as an actuary, Sarah Rowlands trained at Leiths School of Food and Wine in London and then worked in a Michelin-starred restaurant. During this time, her love of flavor and flavor pairings led to her developing a passion for wine. She now works freelance, hosting wine tastings, working at wine fairs, acting as an associate judge for the International Wine and Spirit Competition and an examiner for the Wine Spirit Education Trust, and traveling the world to taste and learn about new and little-known wines. She also gives cookery lessons and bread-making courses.

The Periodic Table of
WINE

FULL-BODIED WHITE

LIGHTER WHITE

1 G **C** Chardonnay: oaked			17 G **Fu** Furmint		28 R **Pp** Picpoul de Pinet	34 R **So** Soave	40 G **Mt** Müller-Thurgau
2 R **Pl** Pessac Léognan	7 G **Gw** Gewürztraminer	12 G **Mu** Muscat	18 R **Vy** Vouvray	23 G **Mc** Muscadet	29 G **Fi** Fiano	35 G **Vd** Verdejo	41 G **Po** Pinot Grigio
3 G **Sé** Sémillon	8 G **Pg** Pinot Gris	13 G **Vi** Viognier	19 G **Ri** Riesling: Alsace or OZ	24 R **Cl** Chablis	30 G **Cb** Chenin Blanc	36 G **Vm** Vermentino	42 G **Al** Albariño
4 G **Mr** Marsanne	9 G **To** Torrontés	14 G **Sb** Sauvignon Blanc	20 G **Ar** Arneis	25 R **Sc** Sancerre	31 G **Vo** Verdelho	37 G **Rs** Riesling: Mosel	43 G **Pa** Parellada
5 R **Mn** Mâcon	10 G **Ro** Roussanne	15 G **Cu** Chardonnay: unoaked	21 **Ga** Gavi	26 R **Gd** Greco di Tufo	32 G **Fa** Falanghina	38 R **Fr** Frascati	44 G **Ve** Verdicchio
6 G **Sv** Sauvignon Blanc: NZ	11 G **Pb** Pinot Blanc	16 G **Ay** Assyrtiko	22 G **Co** Cortese	27 G **Gv** Grüner Veltliner	33 R **Or** Orvieto	39 G **Tr** Trebbiano	45 G **Vv** Vinho Verde

SPARKLING

105 R **As** Asti	106 G **Mo** Moscato	107 R **Pe** Prosecco	108 R **Cv** Cava	109 R **Cr** Crémant

SWEET

113 R **Iw** Icewine	114 R **Vs** Vin Santo	115 R **Tk** Tokaji

FORTIFIED

119 R **Fs** Fino Sherry	120 R **Ol** Oloroso Sherry	121 R **Md** Madeira	122 R **Rm** Rutherglen Muscat	123 G **Px** Pedro Ximénez